MUTUAL BANKING

SHOWING
THE RADICAL DEFICIENCY
OF THE PRESENT CIRCULATING
MEDIUM AND THE ADVANTAGES
OF
A FREE CURRENCY

BY

WILLIAM B. GREENE

PUBLISHED BY

THE REFORM LEAGUE OF DENVER, COLO.

1919

EDITOR'S PREFACE.

THE payment of interest has been opposed by great thinkers in all ages. Philosophers have demonstrated that it has no reason for being. Ethical writers have shown that justice does not countenance it. Economists have proved it an unnecessary evil. Among its greatest opponents we find Aristotle, Berkeley and Proudhon. These three mighty thinkers, though living at different times and in different countries, neither using the same methods of research, or making deductions from the same data, yet, from their various standpoints, reached the conclusion that interest is neither wise, just or necessary. Not all the arguments which any one of these writers employs are used, or would be accepted by either of the others, but to a considerable extent the three reason identically, so that we find Berkeley, the Christian, agreeing with the Pagan, Aristotle, and confirmed by Proudhon, the Rationalist. Of this trio, however, Proudhon alone pointed out that interest could be made to disappear, not by curtailing individual liberty, but only by extending it.

In the main the author of this work follows in Proudhon's path, departing from it in some important particulars, but in general only so modifying his master's work in finance, both critical and constructive, as to make it applicable to the monetary system and economic methods prevailing in the United States. His assault is upon the system of state banks that was in existence when he wrote (nearly half a century ago), and the system of mutual banks by which he proposed to replace it is an adjustment to American routine of the essential principles embodied in Proudhon's "Bank of the People." The reader will have little difficulty in readjusting the arguments to the new conditions resulting from the displacement of the state banks by the national banks.

Analytical examination of Greene's work will show that it is written in elucidation and illumination of the discovery that, considered as a whole, interest payment, as it exists in modern times, is not what it is professed to be, the price paid for the use of borrowed capital, but the premium paid for the insurance of credit. Paying interest is generally accepted as equitable because it is looked upon as a reimbursement of the holder of capital for foregoing the advantage of using his capital himself. Though the so-called borrower really needs capital, and ultimately gets it as a result of the transaction between himself and the so-called lender, this transaction is really not one of borrowing and lending, but simply a temporary exchange of well-known credit for credit less well known, but equally good, and the interest paid is the price of the insurance which the latter credit receives through the exchange. This, under a system of free competition in banking, would fall to cost, or less than 1 per cent per annum. It is now maintained at varying rates, averaging 5 or 6 per cent by giving a monopoly of this exchange of credits to banks, which, in addition to the perfectly sufficient insurance afforded by the centralization of their customers' credit, furnish a supposed extra security by pledging, in a prescribed form, capital belonging to themselves, thus enabling these banks to offer a pretext for charging an exorbitant premium, the power to exact which depends in reality solely upon this monopoly. This book aims at the destruction of their monopoly by allowing perfect freedom in banking, giving to all credit instruments the liberty of such circulation as they can command upon their merits, and thereby enabling producers to monetize their credit directly and at cost, instead of through the mediation of a prescribed and privileged commodity and at an exorbitant price, as well as to increase the circulating power of their credit by methods of organization and insurance similar to that which the author proposes under the name of mutual banking

The long-standing feud between the hard-money advocates and the fiatists has been possible only because each has persisted in looking at only one side of the shield. The former demand a safe currency, the latter desire the benefits of paper money, and each party ignores the other's arguments. This feud the author brings to an end, by proposing a paper currency secured by real property, thus combining the safety of coin with the advantages of paper, and eliminating the evils of both. Whenever a theory of financial reform is broached that involves the issue of paper money, the failures of paper money experiments in the past are brought up as a warning. But the experiments that failed after a fair trial were characterized by one or more of three features which almost inevitably bring disaster, and which mutual banking excludes:

1. The issue of money by a government, or under an exclusive privilege granted by one.

2. The legal tender privilege.

3. Redemption on demand

When the power to issue money is confined to privileged banks, the control of the volume of currency and the rate of interest resides in a cabal, which will sooner or later use its power to drive producers into bankruptcy. When the power to issue money is confined to government itself, losses ultimately ruinous will be suffered through maladministration by incompetence, or by fraud, two factors whose operations, in combination or in alternation, constitute the history of almost all governmental undertakings.

The legal tender privilege adds no virtue to good money, and removes the only effective cure for bad money—the right to reject it. To force bad money on people is as surely disastrous as to force bad food on them. But to dwell at length on this point and on the redemption of notes on demand would anticipate the author's argument.

H. C.

Denver, Colorado, March 1, 1919

MUTUAL BANKING.

CHAPTER I.

THE USURY LAWS.*

ALL USURY LAWS appear to be arbitrary and unjust. Rent paid for the use of all lands and houses is freely determined in the contract between the landlord and tenant; freight is settled by the contract between the shipowner, and the person hiring of him, profit is determined in the contract of purchase and sale. But, when we come to interest on money, principles suddenly change; here the government intervenes and says to the capitalist, "You shall in no case take more than 6 per cent interest on the amount of principal you loan. If competition among capitalists brings down the rate of interest to 3, 2, or 1 per cent, you have no remedy; but if, on the other hand, competition among borrowers forces that rate up to 7, 8 or 9 per cent, you are prohibited, under severe penalties, from taking any advantage of the rise." Where is the morality of this restriction? So long as the competition of the market is permitted to operate without legislative interference, the charge for the use of capital in all or any of its forms will be properly determined by the contracts between capitalists and the persons with whom they deal. If the capitalist charges too much, the borrower obtains money at the proper rate from some other person; if the borrower is unreasonable, the capitalist refuses to part with his money. If lands, houses, bridges, canals, boats, wagons, are abundant in proportion to the demand for them, the charge for the use of them will be proportionally low; if they are scarce, it will be proportionally high. Upon what ground can you justify the legislature in making laws to restrict a particular class of capitalists, depriving them invidiously of the benefit which they would naturally derive from a system of unrestricted competition? If a man owns a sum of money, he must not lend it for more than 6 per cent interest, but he may buy houses, ships, lands, wagons, with it, and these he may freely let out at 50 per cent, if he can find any person willing to pay at that rate. Is not the distinction drawn by the legislature arbitrary, and therefore unjust? A man wishes to obtain certain lands,

---

*This work is a compilation of a series of newspaper articles, hence they are somewhat disconnected, and an occasional repetition will be found.—EDITOR

wagons, etc., and applies to you for money to buy them with; you can lend the money for 6 per cent interest, and no more; but you can purchase the articles the man desires, and let them out to him at any rate of remuneration upon which you mutually agree. Every sound argument in favor of the intervention of the legislature to fix by law the charge for the use of money bears with equal force in favor of legislative intervention to fix by law the rent of lands and houses, the freight of ships, the hire of horses and carriages, or the profit on merchandise sold. Legislative interference, fixing the rate of interest by law, appears, therefore, to be both impolitic and unjust.

EFFECT OF THE REPEAL OF THE USURY LAWS.

But let logic have her perfect work. Suppose the usury laws were repealed today, would justice prevail tomorrow? By no means. The government says to you: "I leave you and your neighbor to compete with each other; fight out your battles between yourselves; I will have nothing more to do with your quarrels." You act upon this hint of the legislature; you enter into competition with your neighbor. But you find the government has lied to you; you find the legislature has no intention of letting you and your neighbor settle your quarrels between yourselves. Far from it, when the struggle attains its height, behold! the government quietly steps up to your antagonist, and furnishes him with a bowie knife and a revolver. How can you, an unarmed man, contend with one to whom the legislature sees fit to furnish bowie knives and revolvers? In fact, you enter the market with your silver dollar, while another man enters the market with his silver dollar. Your dollar is a plain silver dollar, nothing more or nothing less; but his dollar is something very different, for, by permission of the legislature, he can issue bank-bills to the amount of $1.25 and loan money to the extent of double his or your capital. You tell your customer that you can afford to lend your dollar, if he will return it after a certain time, with four cents for the use of it, but that you cannot lend it for anything less. Your neighbor comes between you and your customer, and says to him, "I can do better by you than that. Don't take his dollar on any such terms, for I will lend you a dollar and charge you only three cents for the use of it." Thus he gets your customer away from you; the worst of it is that he still retains another dollar to seduce away the next customer to whom you apply. Nay, more, when he has loaned out his two dollars, he still has 25 cents in specie in his pocket to fall back upon and carry to Texas in case of accident, while you, if you succeed in lending your dollar, must go without money till your debtor pays it back. Yet you and he entered the market, each with a silver dollar; how is it that he thus obtains the advantage over you in every transaction? The BANKING PRIVILEGE which the government has given him, is a murderous weapon against which you cannot contend.

THE USURY LAWS ARE NECESSARY UNDER PRESENT CIRCUMSTANCES

A just balance and just weights? Very well; but if we have an unjust balance, is it not necessary that the weights should be unjust also? A just balance and unjust weights give false measure, and just weights with an unjust balance give false measure in like manner, but an unjust balance and unjust weights* may be so adjust-ed as to give true measure Under our present system, the lender who is not connected with the banks may be oppressed, but the usury laws (unjust as they are when considered without relation to the false system under which we live) afford some protection, at least to the borrower. They are the unjust weights, which, to a certain extent, justify the false balance. It would be well to have a just balance and just weights; that is, it would be well to repeal the usury laws, and to abolish, not only the banking privilege, but also, as we shall proceed to show, the exclusively specie basis of the currency; but it will not do to put new wine into old bottles, nor to mend old garments with new cloth. When the bank lends two dollars, while it owns only one, it gets twice the interest it is actually entitled to. Insist, if you will, upon retaining your peculiar privileges; but consent in the name of moderation and justice, to let me protect myself by the usury laws; for they are not very severe against you after all The usury laws confine you to 6 per cent interest on whatever you loan, but, as the banking laws enable you to loan twice as much as you actually possess, you obtain 12 per cent interest on all the capital you really own. You cannot complain that in your case the usury laws violate, and without due compensation, the right of property, for you only own one dollar, and yet receive interest and transact business, as though you owned two dollars. The usury laws are necessary, not to interfere in your right to your own property, but to limit you in the abuse of the unjust and exclusive privileges granted you by the legislature The antagonism between the usury and the banking laws is like the division of Satan against Satan; and, through their internal conflict and opposition, the modern Hebrew kingdom may one day be brought to destruction

ARGUMENT IN FAVOR OF THE REPEAL OF THE USURY LAWS.

But let us now examine the great argument in favor of the immediate repeal of the usury laws—an argument which, according to those who adduce it, is in every way unanswerable It is said that all the above considerations, though important and certainly to the point, ought to have very little weight in our minds, and that for the following reason: MEN DO, notwithstanding the present laws, take exorbitant interest; and whatever usury laws may be passed, they will continue so to do. If it be acknowledged that it is wrong to take too high interest, that acknowledgement will not help the

---

*Take the STEELYARD for example.

matter, for, though we acknowledge the wrong, we are impotent to prevent it. The usury laws merely add a new evil to one that was bad enough when it was alone. Without a usury law, men will take too high interest; for they have the power to do it as credit is now organized, and no legislation can prevent them; with a usury law they will continue to take unjust interest, and will have recourse to expedients of questionable morality to evade the law. If the taking of too high interest be an evil, is it not still a greater evil for the community to demoralize itself by evading the laws; to demoralize itself by allowing individuals to have recourse to subterranean methods to accomplish an end they are determined to accomplish at all events—an end which they cannot accomplish in the light of day, because of the terror of the law? Thus argue the advocates of immediate repeal, and with much show of reason. There are a hundred ways in which the usury laws may be evaded.

POWER OF CAPITAL IN THE COMMONWEALTH OF MASSACHUSETTS.

We think few persons are aware of the power of capital in this Commonwealth. According to a pamphlet quoted by Mr. Kellogg, containing a list of the wealthy men of Boston, and an estimate of the value of their property, there are 224 individuals in this city who are worth, in the aggregate, $71,855,000; the average wealth of these individuals would be $321,781. In this book, no estimate is made of the wealth of any individual whose property is supposed to amount to less than $100,000. Let us be moderate in our estimates, and suppose that there are, in all the towns and counties in the state, (including Boston), 3,000 other individuals who are worth $30,000 each, their aggregate wealth would amount to $90,000,000. Add to this the $71,855,000 owned by the 224 men, and we have $161,855,000. These estimates are more or less incorrect, but they give the nearest approximation to the truth that we can obtain at the present time. The assessors' valuation of the property in the State of Massachusetts in 1840* was $299,880,338. We find, therefore, by the above estimates, that 3,224 individuals own more than half of all the property in the State. If we suppose each of these 3,224 persons to be the head of a family of five persons, we shall have in all 16,120 individuals. In 1840 the State contained a population of 737,700. Thus 16,120 persons own more property than the remaining 721,580; that is, three persons out of every hundred own more property than the remaining ninety-seven. To be certain that we are within the truth, let us say that six out of every hundred own more property than the remaining ninety-four. These wealthy persons are connected with each other, for the banks are the organization of their mutual relation, and we think, human nature being what it is, that their weight would be brought to bear still more powerfully

---

*This was written before the valuation for 1850 was taken. As the the question is one of principles rather than of figures, we have not conceived it necessary to rewrite the paragraph.

upon the community if the usury laws were repealed. These persons might easily obtain complete control over the banks. They might easily so arrange matters as to allow very little money to be loaned by the banks to any but themselves, and thus they would obtain the power over the money market which a monopoly always gives to those who wield it—that is, they would be able to ask and to obtain pretty much what interest they pleased for their money. Then there would be no remedy; the indignation of the community would be of no avail. What good would it do you to be indignant? You would go indignantly, and pay exorbitant interest, because you would be hard pushed for money. You would get no money at the bank, because it would be all taken up by the heavy capitalists who control those institutions, or by their friends. These would all get money at 6 per cent interest or less, and they would get from you precisely that interest which your necessities might enable them to exact. The usury laws furnish you with some remedy for these evils; for, under those laws, the power of demanding and obtaining illegal interest will be possible only so long as public opinion sees fit to sanction evasions of the statute. As long as the weight of the system is not intolerable to the community, every thing will move quietly; but as soon as the burden of illegal interest becomes intolerable, the laws will be put in force in obedience to the demand of the public, and the evil will be abated to a certain extent. We confess that it is hard for the borrower to be obliged to pay the broker, to pay also for the wear and tear of the lender's conscience, but we think it would be worse for him if a few lenders should obtain a monopoly of the market. And when the usury laws are repealed, what earthly power will exist capable of preventing them from exercising this monopoly? But here an interesting question presents itself "What is the limit of the power of the lender over the borrower?

ACTUAL VALUE AND LEGAL VALUE.

Let us first explain the difference between legal value and actual value.* It is evident, that, if every bank-bill in the country should suddenly be destroyed, no actual value would be destroyed, except perhaps to the extent of the value of so much waste paper. The holders of the bills would lose their money, but the banks would gain the same amount, because they would no longer be liable to be called upon to redeem their bills in specie. Legal value is the legal claim which one man has upon property in the hands of another. No matter how much legal value you destroy, you cannot by that process banish a single dollar's worth of actual value, though you may do a great injustice to individuals. But if you destroy the silver dollars in the banks, you inflict a great loss on the community; for an importation of specie would have to be made to meet the exi-

---

*The reader is requested to notice this distinction between actual and legal value, as we shall have occasion to refer to it again.

gencies of the currency, and this importation would have to be paid for in goods and commodities which are of actual value. When a ship goes down at sea with her cargo on board, so much actual value is lost. But, on the other hand, when an owner loses his ship in some unfortunate speculation, so that the ownership passes from his hands into the hands of some other person, there may be no loss of actual value, as in the case of shipwreck, for the loss may be a mere change of ownership.

The national debt of England exceeds $4,000,000,000 If there were enough gold sovereigns in the world to pay this debt, and these sovereigns should be laid beside each other, touching each other, and in a straight line, the line thus formed would be much more than long enough to furnish a belt of gold extending around the earth. Yet all this debt is mere legal value. If all the obligations by which this debt is held were destroyed, the holders of the debt would become poorer by the amount of legal value destroyed; but those who are bound by the obligations (the tax-paying people of England) would gain to the same amount. Destroy all this legal value, and England would be as rich after the destruction as it was before; because no actual value would have been affected. The destruction of the legal value would merely cause a vast change in the ownership of property; making some classes richer, and, of course, others poorer to precisely the same extent, but if you should destroy actual value to the amount of this debt you would destroy about thirteen times as much actual value (machinery, houses, improvements, products, etc.) as exist at present in the state of Massachusetts. The sudden destruction of $4,000,000,000 worth of actual value would turn the British Islands into a desert. Many persons are unable to account for the vitality of the English government. The secret is partly as follows: The whole property of England is taxed yearly, say three per cent, to pay the interest of the public debt. The amount raised for this purpose is paid over to those who own the obligations which constitute this legal value. The people of England are thus divided into classes, one class is taxed and pays the interest on the debt, the other class receives the interest and lives upon it. The class which receives the interest knows very well that a revolution would be followed by either a repudiation of the national debt, or its immediate payment by means of a ruinous tax on property. This class knows that the nation would be no poorer if the debt were repudiated or paid. It knows that a large portion of the people look upon the debt as being the result of aristocratic obstinacy in carrying on aristocratic wars for the accomplishment of aristocratic purposes. When, therefore, the government wants votes, it looks to this privileged class, when it wants orators and writers, it looks to this same class; when it wants special constables to put down insurrection, it applies to this same class. The people of England pay yearly $120,000,000 (the interest of the debt) to strengthen the hands of a conservative class, whose function it is to prevent all change, and therefore all improvement in the condition of the empire. The owners of the public debt, the pensioners, the holders of sinecure offices, the nobility, and the functionaries of the Established Church, are the Spartans who rule over the English Laconians, Helots, and Slaves. When such powerful support is enlisted in favor of an iniquitous social order, there is very little prospect left of any amelioration in the condition of the people.

THE MATTER BROUGHT NEARER HOME.

But let us bring the matter nearer home. The assessors' valuation of the property in the state of Massachusetts in 1790 was $44,024,349. In 1840 it was $299,880,338. The increase, therefore, during fifty years, was $255,855,989. This is the increase of actual value. If, now, the $44,024,349 which the state possessed in 1790 had been owned by a class, and had been loaned to the community on six months' notes, regularly renewed, at six per cent interest per annum, and the interest, as it fell due, had itself been continually put out at interest on the same terms, that accumulated interest would have amounted in fifty years to $885,524,246. This is the increase of the legal value. A simple comparison will show us that the legal value would have increased three times as fast as the actual value has increased.

Suppose 5,000 men to own $30,000 each; suppose these men to move, with their families, to some desolate place in the state, where there is no opportunity for the profitable pursuit of the occupations either of commerce, agriculture, or manufacturing. The united capital of these 5,000 men would be $150,000,000. Suppose, now, this capital to be safely invested in different parts of the state; suppose these men to be, each of them, heads of families, comprising, on an average, five persons each, this would give us, in all, 25,000 individuals. A servant to each family would give us 5,000 persons more, and these added to the above number would give us 30,000 in all. Suppose, now, that 5,000 mechanics—shoemakers, bakers, butchers, etc.—should settle with their families in the neighborhood of these capitalists, in order to avail themselves of their custom. Allowing five to a family, as before, we have 25,000 to add to the above number. We have, therefore, in all, a city of 55,000 individuals, established in the most desolate part of the state. The people in the rest of the state would have to pay to the capitalists of this city six per cent on $150,000,000 every year; for these capitalists have, by the supposition, this amount out at interest on bond and mortgage, or otherwise. The yearly interest on $150,000,000, at six per cent, is $9,000,000. These wealthy individuals may do no useful work whatever, and, nevertheless, they levy a tax of $9,000,000 per annum on the industry of the state. The tax would be paid in this way. Some money would be brought to the new city, and much produce; the produce would be sold for money to the capitalists, and with the money thus obtained, added to the other, the debtors would pay the interest due. The capitalists would have their choice of the best the state produces, and the mechanics of the city, who receive money from the capitalists, the next choice. Now, how would all this be looked upon by the people of the commonwealth? There would be a general rejoicing over the excellent market for produce which had grown up in so unexpected a place, and the people would suppose the existence of this city of financial horse-leeches to be one of the main pillars of the prosperity of the state

Each of these capitalists would receive yearly $1,800, the interest on $30,000, on which to live Suppose he lives on $900, the half of his income, and lays the other half by to portion off his children as they come to marriageable age, that they may start also with $30,000 capital, even as he did This $900 which he lays by every year would have to be invested. The men of business, the men of talent, in the state, would see it well invested for him. Some intelligent man would discover that a new railroad, canal, or other public work was needed; he would survey the ground, draw a plan of the work, and make an estimate of the expenses; then he would go to this new city and interest the capitalists in the matter The capitalists would furnish money, the people of the state would furnish labor; the people would dig the dirt, hew the wood, and draw the water The intelligent man who devised the plan would receive a salary for superintending the work, the people would receive day's wages, and the capitalists would own the whole; for did they not furnish the money that paid for the construction? Taking a scientific view of the matter, we may suppose the capitalists not to work at all, for the mere fact of their controlling the money would insure all these results We suppose them, therefore, not to work at all; we suppose them to receive, each of them, $1,800 a year; we suppose them to live on one-half of this, or $900, and to lay up the other half for their children. We suppose new-married couples to spring up, in their proper season, out of these families, and that these new couples start, also, each with a capital of $30,000 We ask now, is there no danger of this new city's absorbing unto itself the greater portion of the wealth of the state?

There is no city in this commonwealth that comes fully up to this ideal of a *faineant* and parasite city; but there is no city in the state in which this ideal is not more or less completely embodied.

Suppose, when Virginia was settled in 1607, England had sold the whole territory of the United States to the first settlers for $1,000, and had taken a mortgage for this sum on the whole property. $1,000 at seven per cent per annum, on half-yearly notes, the interest collected and reloaned as it fell due, would amount, in the interval between 1607 and 1850, to $16,777,216,000. All the property in the United States, several times over, would not pay this debt.

If the reader is interested in this matter of the comparative rate of increase of actual and legal value, let him consult the treatise of Edward Kellogg on "Labor and Other Capital," where he will find abundant information on all these points.

How many farmers are there who can give six per cent interest and ultimately pay for a farm they have bought on credit?

THE ANSWER.

What answer, then, shall we return to the question relating to the power of the lender over the borrower? We are forced to answer, that the borrowing community is, under the existing system of credit, VIRTUALLY, according to appearances, in the complete control of the lending community. A considerable time must elapse before this control is actually as well as virtually established, but as the ship in the eddy of the maelstrom is bound to be ultimately ingulfed, so the producer of actual value (if no change is introduced in the system) is bound to be brought into ultimate complete subjection to the holder of legal value.

CHAPTER II.

THE CURRENCY.

Gold and silver are peculiarly adapted to act as a circulating medium. They are: 1. Admitted by common consent to serve for that purpose. 2. They contain within themselves actual intrinsic value, equivalent to the sum for which they circulate, as security against the withdrawal of this consent, or of the public estimation. 3. They lose less by the wear and tear and by the effect of time, than almost any other commodities; and, 4. They are divisible into all and any of the fractional parts into which value may be, or necessarily is, divided. There is no occasion to notice particularly in this place the many other advantages possessed by the precious metals. But we must remember that when we exchange anything for specie we barter one commodity for another. By the adoption of a circulating medium we have facilitated barter, but we have not done away with it—we have not destroyed it. Specie is a valuable commodity and its adoption by society as a medium of exchange does not destroy its character as a purchasable and salable article. Let Peter own a horse; let James own a cow and a pig; let James's cow and pig, taken together, be worth precisely as much as Peter's horse; let Peter and James desire to make an exchange; now, what shall prevent them from making the exchange by direct barter? Again! let Peter own the horse; let James own the cow; and let John own the pig. Peter cannot exchange his horse for the cow, because he would lose by the transaction; neither—and for the same reason—can he exchange it for the pig. The division of the horse would result in the destruction of its value. The hide, it is true, posesses an intrinsic value; and a dead horse makes excellent manure for a grapevine; nevertheless, the division of a horse results in the destruction of its value as a living animal. But if Peter barters his horse with Paul for an equivalent in wheat, what shall prevent him from so dividing his wheat as to qualify himself to offer to James an equivalent for his cow and to John an equivalent for his pig? If Peter trades thus with James and John the transaction is still barter, though the wheat serves as currency and obviates the difficulty in making change. Now, if Paul has gold and silver to dispose of instead of wheat, the gold and silver are still commodities posessing intrinsic value, and every exchange which Paul makes of these for other commodities is always a transaction in barter. There is a great deal of mystification connected with the subject of the currency; but if we remember that, when we sell anything for specie, we buy the specie, and that when we buy anything with specie, we SELL the specie—our ideas will grow wonderfully clear.

THE DISADVANTAGES OF A SPECIE CURRENCY.

The governments of the different nations have made gold and silver a legal tender in the payment of debts. Does this legislation change the nature of the transactions where gold and silver are exchanged for other desirable commodities? Not at all. Does it transform the exchange into something other than barter? By no means. But the exchangeable value of any article depends upon its utility, and the difficulty of obtaining it. Now, the legislatures, by making the precious metals a legal tender enhance their utility in a remarkable manner. It is not their absolute utility, indeed, that is enhanced, but their relative utility in the transactions of trade. As soon as gold and silver are adopted as the legal tender, they are invested with an altogether new utility. By means of this new utility, whoever monopolizes the gold and silver of any country—and the currency, as we shall soon discover, is more easily monopolized than any other commodity—obtains control thenceforth, over the business of that country; for no man can pay his debts without the permission of the party who monopolizes the article of legal tender. Thus, since the courts recognize nothing as money in the payment of debts except the article of legal tender, this party is enabled to levy a tax on all transactions except such as take place without the intervention of credit.

When a man is obliged to barter his commodity for money, in order to have money to barter for such other commodities as he may desire, he at once becomes subject to the impositions which moneyed men know how to practice on one who wants and must have money for the commodity he offers for sale. When a man is called upon suddenly to raise money to pay a debt, the case is still harder. Men whose property far exceeds the amount of their debts in value—men who have much more owing to them than they owe to others—are daily distressed for the want of money; for the want of that intervening medium, which, even when it is obtained in sufficient quantity for the present purposes, acts only as a mere instrument of exchange.

By adopting the precious metals as the legal tender in the payment of debts, society confers a new value upon them, which new value is not inherent in the metals themselves. This new value becomes a marketable commodity. Thus gold and silver become a marketable commodity as (QUOAD) A MEDIUM OF EXCHANGE. This ought not so to be. This new value has no natural measure, because it is not a natural, but a social value. This new social value is inestimable, it is incommensurable with any other known value whatever. Thus money, instead of retaining its proper relative position, becomes a superior species of commodity—superior not in degree, but in kind. Thus money becomes the absolute

king and the demigod of commodities.* Hence follow great social
and political evils. The medium of exchange was not established
for the purpose of creating a new, inestimable, marketable commodity, but for the single end or purpose of facilitating exchanges.
Society established gold and silver as an instrument to mediate between marketable commodities; but what new instrument shall it
create to mediate between the old marketable commodities, and the
new commodity which it has itself called into being? And if it suc-
ceed in creating such new instrument, what mediator can it find for
this new instrument itself, etc.? Here the gulf yawns! No bridge
save that of USURY has been thrown, as yet, over this gulf. Our
exposition is evidently on the brink of the infinite series; we are
marching rapidly forward to the abyss of absurdity. The logicians
know well what the sudden appearance of the infinite series in an
investigation signifies; it signifies the recognition of a phenomenon
and the assigning to it of a mere concomitant, to stand to it in the
place of cause. The phenomenon we here recognize is circulation
or exchange, and we ignore its cause, for we endeavor to account
for it by the movement of specie; which movement is neither circulation nor the cause of circulation. But more of this hereafter. Let
us return to the subject with which we are more immediately concerned; noting, meanwhile, that a specie currency is an absurdity.

THE EVILS OF A SPECIE CURRENCY—USURY.

Society established gold and silver as a circulating medium, in
order that exchanges of commodities might be FACILITATED; but
society made a mistake in so doing; for by this very act it gave to a
certain class of men the power of saying what exchanges shall, and
what exchanges shall not, be FACILITATED by means of this very
circulating medium. The monopolizers of the precious metals have
an undue power over the community; they can say whether money
shall, or shall not, be permitted to exercise its legitimate functions.
These men have a VETO on the action of money, and therefore on
exchanges of commodity; and they will not take off their VETO until they have received usury, or, as it is more politely termed, interest on their money. Here is the great objection to the present currency. Behold the manner in which the absurdity inherent in a
specie currency—or, what is still worse, in a currency of paper
based upon specie—manifests itself in actual operation! The me-
diating value which society hoped would facilitate exchanges becomes an absolute marketable commodity, itself transcending all
reach of mediation. The great natural difficulty which originally
stood in the way of exchanges is now the private property of a
class, and this class cultivate this difficulty, and make money out
of it, even as a farmer cultivates his farm and makes money by his
labor. But there is a difference between the farmer and the usurer;

---

*Money is merchandise just like any other merchandise, precisely as
the TRUMP is a card just like any other card.

for the farmer benefits the community as well as himself, while every dollar made by the usurer is a dollar taken from the pocket of some other individual, since the usurer cultivates nothing but an actual obstruction.

THE MONOPOLY OF THE CURRENCY.

The exigencies of our exposition render it necessary that we should state here three distinct points, as a basis for certain remarks that we propose to submit to the reader:

1. Let us suppose, in order to make a thorough estimate of the amount of money circulating in Massachusetts, that each individual in the state—man, woman, or child—posesses $10 in specie, or in the bills of specie-paying banks. The population of the state was, in the year 1850, about 1,000,000. Our estimate will give us, therefore, about $10,000,000 as the total amount of the circulating medium of the state. This is perhaps a very extravagant supposition; but we desire to make a high estimate, as the greater the amount of the circulating medium, the less will be the force of our objections against the existing currency. Now, since children seldom control any money, our hypothesis apportions to each full-grown person an average of $20—for the children constitute at least one-half of the community; and since women, who constitute one-half of the grown population, generally leave their money with their husbands or fathers, it apportions to each full-grown man an average of $40. We feel confident that the reader will confess, after consulting his pocket-book, that our estimate marks as high as the circumstances of the case will warrant. But to be certain that we do not fall below the truth, let us double the total sum and say that the amount of money circulating in Massachusetts is, on an average, $20,000,000. This is our first point.

2. The valuation of the taxable property existing in the state of Massachusetts, was, for the year 1850, about $600,000,000—or an average of about $600 for every man, woman and child in the state; or an average of about $2,400 for every family of four persons—no contemptible fortune for a workingman! Now, every person of ordinary observation will recognize that this valuation is too high. We are willing to confess that the wealth of the state is unjustly distributed; but we are not willing to confess that the distribution is of the absolutely flagrant character indicated by the valuation; for if a man posessing a mere average amount of wealth, owns property to the value of $600 and a like amount in addition for his wife and for each of his children, where is the immense mass of wealth which the average would apportion to those who actually own less than $600; yes, to those who actually own nothing? We conceive that it is not altogether impossible to penetrate the motives which induced the Valuation Committee to mark the wealth of the State as high as $600,000,000. Indeed we may take occasion as we proceed with our observations to indicate those motives. But let us grant,

for the sake of argument, that the people of Massachusetts, taken as a whole, do actually own property to the value of $600,000,000. Estimating as we have done, the total value of the circulating medium at $20,000,000, it would follow that there is one dollar of currency for every thirty dollars of taxable property. This is our second point.

3. If Mr. Kellogg's statements are worthy of confidence, there are in the city of Boston 224 individuals who are worth, in the aggregate, $71,855,000, or property to the value of about three and one-half times the amount of the whole circulating medium of the commonwealth. This is our third point.

Having stated the three points upon which our reasoning is to turn, we will now suppose that these individuals in Boston, or 224 other persons of equal wealth, residing either in Boston or in other towns or cities in the state, see fit to combine together for the purpose of bringing the whole property of the state ($600,000,000) into their own possession. They may accomplish their object by the following simple process: Let them gradually buy up desirable real estate situated in various parts of the commonwealth, to the value of $40,000,000—double the total amount of the circulating medium. Then let them sell this real estate to different persons, taking mortgages for half of its value on the property, and stipulating that the payments on the mortgages shall be made, all of them, on a certain specified day. Here is the whole story; for mark the consequences! As the day for payment on the mortgages approaches, money will grow scarce, for the reason that the purchasers of the real estate will be preparing themselves to meet the claims upon them; money will, by consequence, rise rapidly in value; trade will be gradually blocked up; and men of undoubted wealth will be closely pressed. If—and they probably will not—but IF the purchasers of the real estate actually pay their debts when the day comes round, then the 224 confederates will have all the money of the state in their hands. Meanwhile the other ordinary debts of the community—debts which arise naturally—will have to be paid also; and money, the only legal tender, will be required in order to effect their payment. But as no money will be obtainable, these last debtors will fail and their property will be sold under the hammer at a fraction of its true value to satisfy their creditors. But who will buy this property? Who besides the 224 confederates will have any available funds? These 224 individuals, by their operation, notwithstanding the losses they will inevitably meet with, will thus obtain control, by means of their $40,000,000—a little less than one-half of their aggregate property—of the greater part of the property of the state. There is no danger that so extensive an operation will ever take place, for transactions like this would convulse society to its foundations, and would necessarily be accompanied by repudiation, revolution and bloodshed. But similar operations on a smaller scale are taking place every day. It is stated in the reports published by the Valuation Committee that the money loaned out at interest and returned as such to the assessors for the year 1850, amounted in the single county of Worcester, to more than $5,000,000—more than one-fourth of the whole circulating medium of the commonwealth. What must have been the consequence if all these debts had happened to fall due at nearly the same time?

You cannot monopolize corn, iron and other commodities, as you can money; for to do so, you would be obliged to stipulate in your sales that payment shall be made to you in those commodities. What a commotion would exist in the community if a company of capitalists should attempt permanently to monopolize all the corn! But money, by the nature of the case, SINCE IT IS THE ONLY LEGAL TENDER, is ALWAYS monopolized. This fact is the foundation of the right of society to limit the rate of interest.

We conclude, therefore, that gold and silver do not furnish a perfect medium of circulation; that they do not furnish facilities for the exchange of ALL commodities. Gold and silver have a value as MONEY, a value which is artificial, and created UNINTENTIONALLY by the act of society establishing the precious metals as a legal tender. This new artificial value overrides all intrinsic actual values, and suffers no mediation between itself and them. Now, money, so far forth as it is mere money, ought to have NO VALUE, and the objection to the use of the precious metals as currency is, that as soon as they are adopted by society as a legal tender, there is superadded to their natural value this new, artificial and unnatural value. Gold and silver cannot facilitate the purchase of this new value which is added to themselves; "a mediator is not a mediator of one." USURY is the characteristic fact of the present system of civilization; and usury depends for its existence upon this superadded, social, unnatural value, which is given artificially to the material of the circulating medium. Destroy the value of this material AS MONEY (not its utility or availability in exchange) and you destroy the possibility of usury. Can this be done so long as material is gold or silver? No.

Whatever is adopted as the medium of exchange should be free from the above-named objections. It should serve the purpose of facilitating ALL exchanges; it should have no value AS MONEY; it should be of such a nature as to permit nothing marketable, nothing that can be bought or sold, to transcend the sphere of its mediation. It should exist in such quantity as to effect all exchanges which may be desirable. It should be co-existent in time and place with such property as is destined for the market. It should be sufficiently abundant and easy of acquirement, to answer all the legitimate purposes of money. It should be capable of being expanded to any extent that may be demanded by the wants of the community; for if the currency be not sufficiently abundant, it retards instead of facilitating exchanges. On the other hand, this medium of exchange should be sufficiently difficult of acquirement to keep it within just limits

Can a currency be devised which shall fulfill all these conditions? Can a currency be adopted which shall keep money always just plenty enough, without suffering it ever to become too plenty? Can such a currency be established on a firm, scientific foundation, so that we may know beforehand that it will work well from the very first moment of its establishment? Can a species of money be found which shall posess EVERY quality which it is desirable that money should have, while it posesses NO quality which it is desirable that money should not have? To all these questions we answer, emphatically, YES!

CHAPTER III.

THE CURRENCY: ITS EVILS AND THEIR REMEDY.

BANK-BILLS are doubly guaranteed. On one side there is the capital of the bank, which is liable for the redemption of the bills in circulation; on the other side are the notes of the debtors of the bank, which notes are (or ought to be, if the bank officers exercise due caution and discretion) a sufficient guaranty for all the bills: for no bills are issued by any bank, except upon notes whereby some responsible person is bound to restore to the bank, after a certain lapse of time, money to the amount borne on the face of the bills. If the notes given by the receivers of the bills are good, then the bills themselves are also good. If we reflect a moment upon these facts, we shall see that a bank of discount and circulation is in reality, two banks in one. There is one bank which does business on the specie capital really paid in, there is another and a very different bank, which does business by issuing bills in exchange for notes whereby the receivers of the bills give security that there shall be paid back by a certain time, money to the amount of the bills issued. Let us now investigate the nature of these two different banks.

THE BUSINESS OF BANKING.

Peter goes into the banking business with one dollar capital, and immediately issues bills to the amount of one dollar and twenty-five cents. Let us say that he issues five bills, each of which is to circulate for the amount of twenty-five cents. James comes to the bank with four of Peter's bills, and says: "Here are four of your new twenty-five cent notes which purport to be payable on demand, and I will thank you to give me a silver dollar for them." Peter redeems the bills and in so doing pays out his whole capital. Afterward comes John, with the fifth note, and makes a demand similar to that lately made by James. Peter answers, slowly and hesitatingly, "I regret—exceedingly—the force of present circumstances; but—I—just paid—out my whole capital—to James. I am —under—the painful necessity—of requesting you—to wait a little longer for your money." John at once becomes indignant and says: "Your bills state on their face that you will pay twenty-five cents upon each one of them whenever they are presented. I present one NOW. Give me the money, therefore, without more words, for my business is urgent this morning." Peter answers: "I shall be in a condition to redeem my bills by the day after tomorrow; but for the meanwhile, my regard for the interest of the public forces me unwillingly to suspend specie payments." "Suspend SPECIE payments!" says John. "What other kind of payment, under Heaven, could you suspend? You agree to pay SPECIE; for specie is the only legal tender and when you don't pay that, you don't pay anything. When you don't pay that YOU BREAK. Why don't you own up at once? But while I am about it I will give you a piece of my mind; this extra note which you have issued beyond your capital is a vain phantom, a hollow humbug and a fraud. And as for your bank, you would better take in your sign; for you have broken." "These be very bitter words," as said the hostess of the Boar's Head Tavern at Eastcheap

John is right Peter's capital is all gone and the note for twenty-five cents, which professes to represent specie in Peter's vaults, represent the tangibility of an empty vision, the shadow of a vacuum. But which bank is it that is broken? Is it the bank that does business on a specie capital, or the bank which does business on the notes of the debtors to the bank? Evidently it is the bank that does business on the specie capital that is broken; it is the specie-paying bank that has ceased to exist.

John understands this very well notwithstanding his violent language a moment since, he knows that his is the only bill which Peter has in circulation, and that Peter owes, consequently, only twenty-five cents; he knows also that the bank has owing to it one dollar and twenty-five cents. Peter owes twenty-five cents and has owing to him a dollar and twenty-five cents. John feels, therefore, perfectly safe. What is John's security? Is it the specie capital? Not at all. James has taken the whole of that. He has for his security the debts which are owing to the bank. Peter's bank begins now to be placed in a sound, philosophical condition. At first he promised to pay one dollar and twenty-five cents in specie, while he actually possessed only one dollar with which to meet the demands that might be made upon him. How could he have made a more unreasonable promise, even if he had tried? Now that he has suspended specie payments, he has escaped from the unphilosophical situation in which he so rashly placed himself. Peter's bank is still in operation—it is by no means broken; his bills are good, guaranteed, and worthy of considerable confidence; only his bank is now a simple and not a complex bank, being no longer two banks in one, for the specie-paying element has vanished in infinite darkness

CURRENCY.

And here we may notice that Peter has solved, after a rough manner indeed, one of the most difficult questions in political economy. His bill for twenty-five cents is CURRENCY, and yet it is not based upon specie, nor directly connected in any way with specie We would request the reader to be patient with us and not make up his mind in regard to our statements until he has read to the end of the chapter; it shall not be very long Light breaks on us here, which we would endeavor to impart to the reader. The security for the bill is legal value, the security in actual value having been carried away by James—that is, the security for the bill is the legal claim which the bank has upon the property of its debtors. We see, therefore, that LEGAL VALUE may be made a basis for the issue of notes to serve as currency; we see, therefore, the faint indication of a means whereby we may perhaps emancipate ourselves from the bondage of hard money, and the worse bondage of paper which pretends to be a representative of hard money.

Let the reader not be alarmed. We abominate banks that suspend specie payment as much as he does. The run of our argument leads us through this desolate valley; but we shall soon emerge into the clear day. Good may come out of this dark region, although we never expected to find it here. For our part, however, we will freely confess, in private to the reader, that we have lately been so accustomed to see good come out of Nazareth that we have acquired the habit of never expecting it from any other quarter. Let us spend a moment, therefore, in exploring this banking Nazareth.

We may notice in considering a bank that has suspended specie payments: 1. The BANK OFFICERS, who are servants of the STOCK-HOLDERS; 2. The BILLS which are issued by the bank-officers, and which circulate in the community as money; and, 3. The NOTES of the debtors of the bank, binding these debtors, which notes, deposited in the safe, are security for the bills issued. Let us now take for illustration, a non-specie-paying bank that shall be "perfect after its kind;" that is a bank whose capital shall be, in ACTUAL value, literally—0. Suppose there are 100 stockholders; suppose $100,000 worth of bills to be in circulation and that $100,000 LEGAL value is secured to the bank by notes given by the bank's debtors. These stockholders will be remarkable individuals, doing business after a very singular fashion. For example. The stockholders own stock in this bank; but as the whole joint stock equals zero, each stock-holder evidently owns only the one-hundredth part of nothing—a species of property that counts much or little, according to the skilfulness with which it is administered. The stockholders, through the agency of the bank-officers, issue their paper, BEARING NO INTEREST; exchanging it for other paper, furnished by those who receive the bills, BEARING INTEREST AT THE RATE OF SIX PER CENT PER ANNUM. The paper received by the bank binds the debtor to the bank to pay interest; while the paper issued by the bank puts it under no obligation to pay any interest at all. Thus the stockholders doing business with no capital whatever, make six per cent per annum on a pretended $100,000 of ACTUAL value which does not exist! Yet, meanwhile, these stockholders furnish the community with an available currency; this fact ought always to be borne in mind. Non-specie-paying banks, of course, make dividends. During the suspension of 1837 and 1838, all the banks of Pennsylvania made dividends, although it was prohibited in the charters of most of them. After the suspension which took place in Philadelphia in October, 1839, most of the banks of that city resolved not to declare dividends until the pleasure of the legislature could be known. By an act authorizing the continuance of the suspension until the 15th of January, 1841, permission was granted to make dividends, contrary to every principle of justice and equity. We do not know why we speak especially of the Pennsylvania banks in this connection; as we have yet to hear of the first bank, either in Pennsylvania or in any other State, that has had the delicacy to suspend the declaration of dividends merely because it suspended specie payments.

THE MUTUAL BANK.

Our non-specie-paying bank being in the interesting position described, let us inquire whether it is not in the process of bringing forth something which shall be entirely different from itself. We ask first, why a non-specie-paying bank should be permitted to make dividends. Its bills are perfectly good, whether the bank have any capital or not, provided the officers exercise due discretion in discounting notes; and it is evident that the stockholders have no right to ask to be paid for the use of their capital, since the capital in question ought to be specie, which they confess, by suspending specie payments, that they do not furnish But if no dividends are to be declared, what are we to do with the immense amount of interest-money that will accumulate in the bank. Our answer to this question is so simple that we are almost ashamed to state it. Justice requires that all the interest-money accumulated —so much only excepted as is required to pay the expenses of the institution and the average of loss by bad debts—should be paid back to the borrowers in the proportion of the business which they have individually done with the bank. But since it would be by no means easy, practically, to thus pay the extra interest-money back, it would be better for the bank to turn the difficulty by lending its money at precisely that rate of interest and no more, say one per cent per annum, which would suffice to pay the expenses of the institution, including the average loss by bad debts. A bank of this character would be a MUTUAL BANK. This is not the institution we advocate and of which we propose to submit a plan to the reader; but it will serve in this place for the purposes of illustration. A bank that suspends specie payments may present two evident advantages to the community—first, it may furnish a currency; second, it may loan out its bills at one per cent interest per annum. That such a bank may furnish currency is proved by abundant experience, for suspending banks go right on with their business, and that their money circulates well is proved by the fact that such banks have hitherto seldom failed to declare good dividends. That they may loan their money at one per cent interest per annum is shown by the fact that the old banks do not pay more than one per cent per annum for their expenses, including losses by bad debts, and that the guaranty of the new bills consists in the excellence of the notes furnished by the borrower, so that, if there is anything to be paid for this guaranty, it ought to be paid to the borrower himself, and not to any other person. We will not prolong this exposition, since a multiplicity of words would serve only to darken the subject. We invite the reader to reflect for himself upon the matter and to form his own conclusions. We repeat that we do not advocate a bank of the nature here described, since we conceive that such an institution would be eminently unsafe and dangerous, and for a hundred reasons among which may be counted the inordinate power that would be conferred on the bank's officers; but, as we said before, it may serve for illustration. Neither do we propose this plan as a theoretical solution of the difficulties noticed in the preceeding chapters as inseparable from the existing currency. We reserve our own plan, and shall submit it to the reader at the end of the next chapter.

CHAPTER IV.

MUTUAL BANKING.

In the title-page of a book on "Money and Banking,*" published at Cincinnati, the name of William Beck appears, not as author, but as publisher; yet there is internal evidence in the book sufficient to prove that Mr. Beck is the author. But who was or is Mr Beck? What were his experience and history? Is he still living? No one appears to know. He seems to stand like one of Ossian's heroes, surrounded with clouds, solitude and mystery. In the pages of Proudhon, socialism appears as an avenging fury, clothed in garments dipped in the sulphur of the bottomless pit and armed for the punishment of imbeciles, liars, scoundrels, cowards and tyrants; in those of Mr. Beck, she presents herself as a constructive and beneficent genius, the rays of her heavenly glory intercepted by a double veil of simplicity and modesty. Mr. Beck's style has none of the infernal fire and profanity which cause the reader of the "Contradictions Economiques" to shudder; you seek in vain in his sentences for the vigor and intense self-consciousness of Proudhon; yet the thoughts of Proudhon are there. One would suppose from the naturalness of his manner, that he was altogether ignorant of the novelty and true magnitude of his ideas.

MR. BECK'S BANK.

In Mr. Beck's plan for a Mutual Bank—which consists in a simple generalization of the system of credit in account that is well described in the following extract from J. Stuart Mill's "Political Economy"—there is one fault only; but that fault is fatal; it is that the people can never be induced to adopt the complicated method of accounts which would be rendered necessary:

"A mode of making credit answer the purposes of money, by which, when carried far enough, money may be very completely superseded, consists in making payments by checks. The custom of keeping the spare cash reserved for immediate use or against contingent demands, in the hands of a banker and making all payments, except small ones, by orders on bankers, is in this country spreading to a continually larger portion of the public. If the person making the payment and the person receiving it kept their money with the same banker, the payment would take place without any intervention of money, by the mere transfer of its amount

---

*"Money and Banking, or Their Nature and Effects Considered; Together With a Plan for the Universal Diffusion of Their Legitimate Benefits Without Their Evils." By A Citizen of Ohio Cincinnati: Published by William Beck, 1839 ; 16mo, pp. 212.

in the banker's books from the credit of the payer to that of the receiver. If all persons in London kept their cash at the same banker's and made all their payments by means of checks, no money would be required or used for any transactions beginning and terminating in London. This ideal limit is almost attained in fact, so far as regards transactions between dealers. It is chiefly in the retail transactions between dealers and consumers, and in the payment of wages, that money or bank-notes now pass and then only when the amounts are small. In London, even shop-keepers of any amount of capital, or extent of business, have generally an account with a banker, which, besides the safety and convenience of the practice, is to their advantage in another respect, by giving them an understood claim to have their bills discounted in cases where they could not otherwise expect it. As for the merchants and larger dealers, they habitually make all payments in the course of their business, by checks. They do not, however, all deal with the same banker; and when A gives a check to B, B usually pays it, not into the same, but into another bank. But the convenience of business has given birth to an arrangement which makes all the banking-houses of the City of London, for certain purposes, virtually one establishment. A banker does not send the checks which are paid into his banking-house to the banks on which they are drawn and demand money for them. There is a building called the Clearing House, to which every city banker sends each afternoon, all the checks on other bankers which he has received during the day; and they are there exchanged for the checks on him which have come into the hands of other bankers, the balances only being paid in money. By this contrivance, all the business transactions of the City of London during that day amounting often to millions of pounds and a vast amount besides of country transactions, represented by bills which country bankers have drawn upon their London correspondents, all liquidated by payments not exceeding, on the average, £200,000."—(Vol. ii., p. 47).

"Money," says Mr. Beck, "follows in the track of claim. Its progress is the discharge and satisfaction of claim. The payment of money is effectually the discharge of the debtor; but it is not equally effectual in satisfaction of the creditor. Though it releases the debtor, it still leaves the creditor to seek the real object of his desire. It does not put him in possession of it, but of something which enables him to obtain it. He must exchange this money by purchase for the article he wants before that object is attained. In payment of debts, it passes from claimant to claimant, discharging and paying claims as it goes. Money follows claim; both continually revolving through all classes of society in repeated and perpetual circles, constantly returning to their several stations, drawn thither by operations of industry or of business.

"In the possession of money every one has his turn. It comes to him in the shape of payment for his sales or his industry and passes from him in the shape of payment or expenditure, again to return at its proper time and on a proper occasion to serve the same purposes as before.

"Now, I contend that as the progress of money lies in a circular route, a certain system of account may be made to supply its place, where its track and extent can, in that circle, be included and distinguished.

"By a CIRCLE, I mean that range of society which includes the whole circulating movement of money, with the accompanying causes and effects of its progress; viz, claims, debts and payments; so that, if we wish to trace its path, every point of that path will be contained within it. Such is the great circle of society. This contains the whole body of debtors and the whole body of creditors. It contains all the debtors to the creditors and all the creditors to the debtors. All would be included in the jurisdiction of a power that by any possibility could preside over the whole. Creditors are sellers; debtors are buyers. But no man continually sells without sometimes buying, nor does any man continually buy without sometimes selling. The creditor who receives money from his debtor, again expends this money upon others, who thereby, in their turns, become creditors and receive their money back again. All these movements are within the range of the one circle of society. Now, it is evident that if an account were kept by a presiding power, the goods which any person receives, being of equal value, would pay for those which he had previously delivered; would replace him in his original assests and cancel the obligation to him without the aid of money. Hence, after the whole process, it would seem that the intermediate passage and return of money were superfluous. If the dealings are not directly backward and forward—that is, between one creditor and his debtor and back again from the same debtor to the same creditor—the effect will be the same; for as this whole circle includes every creditor, every debtor and in fact every individual in that society, so it contains every account to which the claims of any creditor would apply, and every account to which the same creditor would be indebted. The agency of the presiding power would render it *pro forma,* the representative to every creditor of his individual debtor; and to every debtor, the representative of his individual creditor. It would form a common center for all claims by every creditor on his debtor. It would form the channel for the discharge of his debts and the receipt of his claims. It would show the state of his account with society, and the balance, if in favor, would be available as so much cash.

"This is what is meant by a CIRCLE. Such is the great circle of society, the only one which is complete and perfect, and such are the advantages contained in it.

"Hence the plan I propose is adapted to this circle, to exhibit the revolving track of money within it; to contain the several points of its progress; and, at each of these points, to perform its duty and supply its place by the revolution of debits and credits in account, instead of the revolutions of the actual material money."

There are many practical processes by which the business-world make credit perform the functions of money, among which may be especially noticed—first, that by credit in account, and second, that by bills of exchange. Mr, Beck thought out a Mutual Bank by generalizing credit in account; Proudhon, by generalizing the bill of exchange

BILLS OF EXCHANGE.

Let it be supposed that there are ten shoe-manufacturers in Lynn, who sell their shoes to ten shopkeepers in Boston; let it be supposed, also, that there are ten wholesale grocers in Boston who furnish goods to ten retail grocers in Lynn. If the value of the shoes equals the value of the groceries, the ten retail grocers in Lynn would have no occasion to send money to Boston to pay their indebtedness to the wholesale grocers; neither would the ten shopkeepers in Boston have occasion to send money to Lynn to discharge their debt to the ten shoe manufacturers; for the Lynn retail grocers might pay the money to the the Lynn shoe-manufacturers; these shoe-manufacturers writing to the Boston shopkeepers, who are their debtors, requesting them to pay the Boston wholesale grocers, who are the creditors of the Lynn retail grocers It is very possible that the transactions of all these persons with each other might be settled in this way without the transmission of any money either from Boston to Lynn, or from Lynn to Boston. The transfer of debts in the process here indicated gives rise to what are called, in mercantile language, drafts, or bills of exchange; though regular bills of exchange are seldom drawn in this country, except against foreign account. A bill of exchange reads generally somewhat as follows:

"To Mr. E. F.——days after sight, on this my FIRST bill of exchange (second and third of the same date and tenor not paid) pay to A. B., without further advice from me, —— dollars, value received, and charge the same to account of your obedient servant, C. D "

This form evidently implies that the bill is made out in triplicates. The bill must also, of course be dated. A DRAFT is a bill of exchange drawn up with the omission of some of the solemnity and particularity of the regular bill.

Bills of exchange are useful, not only for the payment of debts at distant places without transportation of the precious metals, but also as a means by which a debt due from one person may be made available for OBTAINING CREDIT from another. It is usual in every trade to give a certain length of credit for goods bought—ninety days, six months, eight months, or a longer time, as may be determined by the convenience of the parties, or by the custom of the particular trade and place. If a man has sold goods to another on six month's credit, he may draw a bill upon his debtor, payable in six months, get his bill discounted at the bank and thus qualify himself to purchase such things as he may require in his business, without waiting for the six months to expire. But bills of exchange do more than this. They not only obviate, upon occasions, the necessity for ready money; they not only enable a man to command ready money before the debts due to him arrive at maturity; they often actually take place and perform the functions of money itself. J. Stuart Mill, quoting from Mr, Thornton, says: "Let us imagine a farmer in the country to discharge a debt of £10 to his neighboring grocer, by giving him a bill for that sum, drawn on his corn-factor in London, for grain sold in the metropolis; and the grocer to transmit the bill—he having previously indorsed it—to a neighboring sugar-baker in discharge of a like debt; and the sugar-baker to send it when again indorsed, to a West India merchant in an outport; and the West India merchant to deliver it to his country banker, who also indorses it and sends it into further circulation. The bill will in this case have effected five payments, exactly as if it were a £10 note payable to bearer on demand. A multitude of bills pass between trader and trader in the country in the manner which has been described, and they evidently form in the strictest sense, a part of the circulating medium of the kingdom" Mr. Mill adds: "Many bills, both domestic and foreign, are at last presented for payment quite covered with indorsements, each of which represents either a fresh discounting, or a pecuniary transaction in which the bill has performed the functions of money. Up to twenty years ago, the circulating medium of Lancashire for sums above £5 was almost entirely composed of such bills."

In our explanation of the system of banking which results from a generalization of the bill of exchange, we will let the master speak for himself.

PROUDHON'S BANK.

"We must destroy the royalty of gold; we must republicanize specie, by making every product of labor ready money.

"Let no one be frightened beforehand. I by no means propose to reproduce under a rejuvenated form, the old ideas of paper money, money of paper, assignats, bank-bills, etc., etc.; for all these palliatives have been known, tried and rejected long ago. These representations on paper, by which men have believed themselves able to replace the absent god, are, all of them, nothing other than a homage paid to metal—an adoration of metal, which has been always present to men's minds, and which has always been taken by them as the measure or evaluator of products.

"Everybody knows what a bill of exchange is. The creditor requests the debtor to pay to him, or to his order, at such a place, at such a date, such a sum of money.

"The promissory note is the bill of exchange inverted; the debtor promises the creditor that he will pay, etc.

" 'The bill of exchange,' says the statute, 'is drawn from one place on another. It is dated. It announces the sum to be paid;

the time and place where the payment is to be made; the value to be furnished in specie, in merchandise, in account, or in other form It is to the order of a third person, or to the order of the drawer himself. If it is by 1st, 2nd, 3rd, 4th, etc., it must be so stated.'

"The bill of exchange supposes, therefore, exchange, provision and acceptance; that is to say, a value created and delivered by the drawer; the existence, in the hands of the drawee, of the funds destined to acquit the bill, and the promise on the part of the drawee, to acquit it. When the bill of exchange is clothed with all these formalities; when it represents a real service actually rendered, or merchandise delivered; when the drawer and drawee are known and solvent; when, in a word, it is clothed with all the conditions necessary to guarantee the accomplishment of the obligation, the bill of exchange is considered GOOD; it circulates in the mercantile world like bank-paper, like specie. No one objects to receiving it under pretext that a bill of exchange is nothing but a piece of paper. Only—since, at the end of its circulation, the bill of exchange, before being destroyed, must be exchanged for specie—it pays to specie a sort of seigniorial duty, called DISCOUNT.

"That which, in general, renders the bill of exchange insecure, is precisely this promise of final conversion into specie; and thus the idea of metal like a corrupting royalty, infects even the bill of exchange and takes from it its certainty

"Now, the whole problem of the circulation consists in generalizing the bill of exchange; that is to say, in making of it an anonymous title, exchangeable forever, and redeemable at sight, but only in merchandise and services

"Or, to speak a language more comprehensible to financial adepts, the problem of the circulation consists in BASING bank-paper, not upon specie, nor bullion, nor immovable property, which can never produce anything but a miserable oscillation between usury and bankruptcy, between the five-franc piece and the assignat; but by basing it upon PRODUCTS.

"I conceive this generalization of the bill of exchange as follows:

"A hundred thousand manufacturers, miners, merchants, commissioners, public carriers, agriculturists, etc., throughout France, unite with each other in obedience to the summons of the the the government and by simple authentic declaration, inserted in the 'Moniteur' newspaper, bind themselves respectively and reciprocally to adhere to the statutes of the Bank of Exchange; which shall be no other than the Bank of France itself, with its constitution and attributes modified on the following basis:

"1st. The Bank of France, become the Bank of Exchange, is an institution of public interest. It is placed under the guardianship of the state and is directed by delegates from all the branches of Industry.

"2nd. Every subscriber shall have an account open at the

Bank of Exchange for the discount of his business paper; and he shall be served to the same extent as he would have been under the conditions of discount in specie; that is, in the known measure of his faculties, the business he does, the positive guarantees he offers, the real credit he might reasonably have enjoyed under the old system.

"3rd. The discount of ordinary commercial paper, whether of drafts, orders, bills of exchange, notes on demand, will be made in bills of the Bank of Exchange, of denominations of 25, 50, 100 and 1,000 francs.

"Specie will be used in making change only.

"4th. The rate of discount will be fixed at —— per cent, commission included, no matter how long the paper has to run. With the Bank of Exchange all business will be finished on the spot.

"5th. Every subscriber binds himself to receive in all payments, from whomsoever it may be and at par, the paper of the Bank of Exchange.

"6th. Provisionally and by way of transition, gold and silver coin will be received in exchange for the paper of the bank, and at their nominal value.

"Is this a paper currency?

"I answer unhesitatingly, No! It is neither paper-money, nor money of paper, it is neither government checks, nor even bank-bills; it is not of the nature of anything that has been hitherto invented to make up for the scarcity of the specie. It is the bill of exchange generalized.

"The essence of the bill of exchange is constituted—first, by its being drawn from one place on another; second, by its representing a real value equal to the sum it expresses; third, by the promise or obligation on the part of the drawee to pay it when it falls due.

"In three words, that which constitutes the bill of exchange is exchange, provision, acceptance.

"As to the date of issue, or of falling due; as to the designation of the places, persons, object—these are particular circumstances which do not relate to the essence of the title, but which serve merely to give it a determinate personal and local actuality.

"Now, what is the bank-paper I propose to create?

"It is the bill of exchange stripped of the circumstantial qualities of date, place, person, object, term of maturity, and reduced to its essential qualities—exchange, acceptance, provision.

"It is, to explain myself still more clearly, the bill of exchange, payable at sight and forever, drawn from every place in France upon every other place in France, made by 100,000 drawers, guaranteed by 100,000 indorsers, accepted by the 100,000 subscribers drawn upon; having provision made for its payment in the 100,000 work-shops, manufactories, stores, etc., of the same 100,000 subscribers.

"I say, therefore, that such a title unites every condition of solidity and security and that it is susceptible of no depreciation.

"It is eminently solid; since on one side it represents the ordinary, local, personal, actual paper of exchange, determined in its object and representing a real value, a service rendered, merchandise delivered, or whose delivery is guaranteed and certain; while on the other side it is guaranteed by the contract, *in solido,* of 100,-000 exchangers, who, by their mass, their independence, and at the same time by the unity and connection of their operations, offer millions of millions of probability of payment against one of non-payment. Gold is a thousand times less sure.

"In fact, if in the ordinary conditions of commerce, we may say that a bill of exchange made by a known merchant offers two chances of payment against one of non-payment, the same bill of exchange, if it is indorsed by another known merchant, will offer four chances of payment against one. If it is indorsed by three, four or a greater number of merchants equally well known, there will be eight, sixteen, thirty-two, etc., to wager against one that three, four, five, etc., known merchants will not fail at the same time, since the favorable chances increase in geometrical proportion with the number of indorsers. What, then, ought to be the certainty of a bill of exchange made by 100,000 well-known subscribers, who are all of them interested to promote its circulation?

"I add that this title is susceptible of no depreciation. The reason for this is found, first, in the perfect solidity of a mass of 100,000 signers. But there exists another reason, more direct, and if possible, more reassuring: it is that the issues of the new paper can never be exaggerated like those of ordinary bank-bills, treasury notes, paper money, assignats, etc., for the issues take place against good, commercial paper only, and in the regular, necessarily limited, measured and proportionate process of discounting.

"In the combination I propose, the paper (at once sign of credit and instrument of circulation) grows out of the best business-paper, which itself represents products delivered, and by no means merchandise unsold. This paper, I affirm, can never be refused in payment, since it is subscribed beforehand by the mass of producers.

"This paper offers so much the more security and convenience, inasmuch as it may be tried on a small scale, and with as few persons as you see fit, and that without the least violence, without the least peril.

"Suppose the Bank of Exchange to start at first on a basis of 1,000 subscribers instead of 100,000; the amount of paper it would issue would be in proportion to the business of these 1,000 subscribers, and negotiable only among themselves. Afterwards, according as other persons should adhere to the bank, the proportion of bills would be as 5,000, 10,000, 50,000, etc, and their circulation would grow with the number of subscribers, as a money peculiar to them. Then, when the whole of France should have adhered to the stat-

utes of the new bank, the issue of paper would be equal, at every
instant, to the the totality of circulating values.

"I do not conceive it necessary to insist longer. Men acquainted
with banking will understand me without difficulty, and will supply from their own minds the details of execution.

"As for the vulgar, who judge of all things by the material aspect,
nothing for them is so similar to an assignat as a bill of the Bank of
Exchange. For the economist, who searches the idea to the bot-
tom, nothing is so different. They are two titles, which, under the
same matter, the same form, the same denomination, are diamet-
rically opposed to each other."—(*Organization du Credit de la
Circulation—Banque d'Exchange;* p. 23).

REMARKS.

We have several objections to Proudhon's bank. We propose
them with diffidence, as Proudhon has undoubtedly prepared an
adequate answer to them. Nevertheless, as he has not given that
answer in his writings, we have a right to state them. They are as
follows:

1st. We ask M. Proudhon how he would punish arbitrary con-
duct, partiality, favoritism and self-sufficiency, on the part of the
officers of his bank. When we go to the mutual bank to borrow
money, we desire to be treated politely and to receive fair play.

2nd. We ask him how he would prevent intriguing members
from caballing to obtain control of the direction; or how he would
prevent such intrigues from bringing forth evil results.

3rd. We ask him how he would prevent the same property,
through the operation of successive sales, from being represented,
at the same time, by several different bills of exchange, all of
which are liable to be presented for discount. For example. Suppose Peter sells John $100 worth of pork at six months credit and
takes a bill at six months for it; and that John sells afterward this
same pork to James at a like credit, taking a like bill; what shall
prevent both Peter and John from presenting their bills for discount? Both bills are REAL bills, resulting from sales actually
effected. Neither of them can be characterized as fictitious paper,
and meanwhile, only one represents actual property. The same
barrel of pork, by being sold and resold at credit one hundred times
will give rise to one hundred real bills. But is it not absurd to
say that the bank is safe in discounting all this paper, for the reason that it is entirely composed of real bills, when we know only
one of them represents the barrel of pork? It follows, therefore,
that not every real bill is adequately guaranteed. How, then, can
Proudhon be certain that his issues of bank-paper "will never be
exaggerated?"

4th. We ask him how he would cause his bank to operate to
the decentralization of the money power.

For ourselves, we submit (and for the reason that it is necessary
to have some system that obviates the foregoing objections) that

the issues of mutual money ought—at least, here in New England, the theory of Proudhon to the contrary notwithstanding—to be related to a basis of determinate actual property.

Our plan for a Mutual Bank is as follows:

1st. Any person, by pledging actual property to the bank, may become a member of the Mutual Banking Company.

2nd. Any member may borrow the paper money of the bank on his own note running to maturity (without indorsement) to an amount not to exceed one-half of the value of the property by himself pledged.

3rd. Each member binds himself in legal form, on admission, to receive in all payments, from whomsoever it may be and at par, the paper of the Mutual Bank.

4th. The rate of interest at which said money shall be loaned shall be determined by, and shall if possible, just meet and cover, the bare expenses of the institution. As for interest in the common acceptation of the word, its rate shall be at the Mutual Bank precisely 0.

5th No money shall be loaned to any persons who are not members of the company; that is, no money shall be loaned, except on a pledge of actual property.

6th. Any member, by paying his debts to the bank, may have his property released from pledge, and be himself released from all obligations to the bank, or to the holders of the bank's money, as such.

7th. As for the bank, it shall never redeem any of its notes in specie; nor shall it ever receive specie in payments, or the bills of specie-paying banks, except at a discount of one-half of one per cent.

Ships and houses that are insured, machinery, in short, anything that may be sold under the hammer, may be made a basis for the issue of mutual money. Mutual Banking opens the way to no monopoly; for it simply elevates every species of property to the rank which has hitherto been exclusively occupied by gold and silver. It may be well (we think it will be necessary) to begin with real estate; we do not say it would be well to end there!

CHAPTER V.

To the Honorable the Senate and House of Representatives of the Commonwealth of Massachusetts.

THIS prayer of your petitioners humbly showeth, that the farmers, mechanics and other actual producers, whose names are hereunto subscribed, believe the present organization of the currency to be unjust and oppressive. They, therefore, respectfully request your honorable body to republicanize gold, silver and bank-bills, by the enactment of a GENERAL MUTUAL BANKING LAW.

A law, embracing the following provisions, would be eminently satisfactory to your petitioners:

1. The inhabitants or any portion of the inhabitants, of any town or city in the Commonwealth may organize themselves into a Mutual Banking Company.

2. Any person may become a member of the Mutual Banking Company of any particular town, by pledging REAL ESTATE situated in that town, or in its immediate neighborhood, to the Mutual Bank of that town.

3. The Mutual Bank of any town may issue PAPER-MONEY to circulate as currency among persons willing to employ it as such.

4. Every member of a Mutual Banking Company shall bind himself, and be bound, in due legal form, on admission, to receive in payment of debts, at par, and from all persons, the bills issued, and to be issued, by the particular Mutual Bank to which he may belong; but no member shall be obliged to receive, or have in possession, bills of said Mutual Bank to an amount exceeding the whole value of the property pledged by him.

5. Any member may borrow the paper money of the bank to which he belongs, on his own note running to maturity (without indorsement), to an amount not to exceed one-half of the value of the property pledged by him.

6. The rate of interest at which said money shall be loaned by the bank, shall be determined by, and shall, if possible, just meet and cover the bare expenses of the institution.

7. No money shall be loaned by the bank to persons who do not become members of the company by pledging real estate to the bank.

8. Any member, by paying his debts to the Mutual Bank to which he belongs, may have his property released from pledge, and be himself released from all obligations to said Mutual Bank, and to holders of the Mutual-Bank money, as such.

9. No Mutual Bank shall receive other than Mutual-Bank paper-money in payment of debts due to it, except at a discount of one-half of one per cent.

10. The Mutual Banks of the several counties in the Commonwealth shall be authorized to enter into such arrangements with each other as shall enable them to receive each other's bills in payments of debts; so that, for example, a Fitchburg man may pay his debts to the Barre Bank in Oxford money, or in such other Worcester-county money as may suit his convenience.

REMARKS.

Let A, B, C, D and E take a mortgage upon real estate owned by F, to cover a value of, say, $600; in consideration of which mortgage, let A, B, C, D and E, who are timber-dealers, hardware merchants, carpenters, masons, painters, etc., furnish planks, boards, shingles, nails, hinges, locks, carpenters' and masons' labor, etc., to the value of $600, to F, who is building a house. Let the mortgage have six months to run. A, B, C, D and E are perfectly safe; for either F pays at the end of the six months, and then the whole transaction is closed; or F does not pay, and then they sell the real estate mortgaged by him, which is worth much more than $600, and pay themselves, thus closing the transaction. This transaction, generalized, gives the Mutual Bank, and furnishes a currency based upon products and services, entirely independent of hard money, or paper based on hard money. For A, B, C, D and E may give to F, instead of boards, nails, shingles, etc., 600 certificates of his mortgage, said certificates being receivable by them for services and products, each one in lieu of a silver dollar; each certificate being, therefore, in all purchases from them, equivalent to a one-dollar bill. If A, B, C, D and E agree to receive these certificates, each one in lieu of a silver dollar, for the redemption of the mortgage; if, moreover, they agree to receive them, each one in lieu of a silver dollar, from whomsoever it may be, in all payments—then A, B, C, D and E are a banking company that issues mutual money; and as they never issue money except upon a mortgage of property of double the value of the money issued, their transactions are always absolutely safe, and their money is always absolutely good.

Any community that embraces members of all trades and professions may totally abolish the use of hard money, and of paper based on hard money, substituting mutual money in its stead; and they may always substitute mutual money in the stead of hard money and bank bills, to the precise extent of their ability to live within themselves on their own resources.

THE RATE OF INTEREST.

As interest-money charged by Mutual Banks covers nothing but the expenses of the institutions, such banks may lend money, at A RATE OF LESS THAN ONE PER CENT PER ANNUM, to persons offering good security.

ADVANTAGES OF MUTUAL BANKING.

It may be asked "What advantage does mutual banking hold out to individuals who have no real estate to offer in pledge?" We answer this question by another: What advantage do the existing banks hold out to individuals who desire to borrow, but are unable to offer adequate security? If we knew of a plan whereby, through an act of the legislature, every member of the community might be made rich, we would destroy this petition, and draw up another embodying that plan. Meanwhile, we affirm that no system was ever devised so beneficial to the poor as the system of mutual banking; for if a man having nothing to offer in pledge, has a friend who is a farmer, or other holder of real estate, and that friend is willing to furnish security for him, he can borrow money at the mutual bank at a rate of 1 per cent interest a year; whereas, if he should borrow at the existing banks, he would be obliged to pay 6 per cent. Again, as mutual banking will make money exceedingly plenty, it will cause a rise in the rate of wages, thus benefiting the man who has no property but his bodily strength; and it will not cause a proportionate increase in the price of the necessaries of life: for the price of provisions, etc., depends on supply and demand; and mutual banking operates, not directly on supply and demand, but to the diminution of the rate of interest on the medium of exchange. Mutual banking will indeed cause a certain rise in the price of commodities by creating a new demand; for, with mutual money, the poorer classes will be able to purchase articles which, under the present currency, they never dream of buying.

But certain mechanics and farmers say, "We borrow no money, and therefore pay no interest. How, then, does this thing concern us?" Hearken, my friends! let us reason together. I have an impression on my mind that it is precisely the class who have no dealings with the banks, and derive no advantages from them, that ultimately pay all the interest money that is paid. When a manufacturer borrows money to carry on his business, he counts the interest he pays as a part of his expenses, and therefore adds the amount of interest to the price of his goods. The consumer who buys the goods pays the interest when he pays for the goods; and who is the consumer, if not the mechanic and the farmer? If a manufacturer could borrow money at 1 per cent, he could afford to undersell all his competitors, to the manifest advantage of the farmer and mechanic. The manufacturer would neither gain nor lose; the farmer and mechanic, who have no dealings with the bank, would gain the whole difference; and the bank—which, were it not for the competition of the Mutual Bank, would have loaned the money at 6 per cent interest—would lose the whole difference. It is the indirect relation of the bank to the farmer and mechanic, and not its direct relation to the manufacturer and merchant, that enables it to make money. When foreign competition prevents the manufacturer from keeping up the price of his goods, the farmer and mechanic, who

are consumers, do not pay the interest-money: but still the interest
is paid by the class that derive no benefit from the banks; for, in
this case, the manufacturer will save himself from loss by cutting
down the wages of his workmen who are producers. Wages fluc-
tuate, rising and falling (other things being equal) as the rate of
interest falls or rises. If the farmer, mechanic and operative are
not interested in the matter of banking, we know not who is.

MUTUAL MONEY IS GENERALLY COMPETENT TO FORCE ITS OWN WAY INTO GENERAL CIRCULATION

Let us suppose the Mutual Bank to be at first established in a
single town, and its circulation to be confined within the limits of
that town. The trader who sells the produce of that town in the
city and buys there such commodities—tea, coffee, sugar, calico,
etc.—as are required for the consumption of his neighbors, sells and
buys on credit. He does not pay the farmer cash for his produce;
he does not sell that produce for cash in the city; neither does he
buy his groceries, etc., for cash from the city merchant: but he
buys of the farmer at, say, eight months' credit; and he sells to
the city merchant at, say, six months' credit. He finds, moreover, as a general thing, that the exports of the town which pass
through his hands very nearly balance the imports that he brings
into the town for sale; so that, in reality, the exports—butter,
cheese, pork, beef, eggs, etc.—pay for the imports—coffee, sugar,
etc. And how, indeed, could it be otherwise? It is not to be supposed that the town has silver mines and a mint; and, if the people
pay for their imports in money, it will be because they have become enabled so to do by selling their produce for money. It follows, therefore, that the people in a country town do not make the
money, whereby they pay for store-goods, off each other, but that
they make it by selling their produce out of the town. There are,
therefore, two kinds of trading going on at the same time in the
town—one trade of the inhabitants with each other; and another
of the inhabitants, through the store, with individuals living out of
town. And these two kinds of trade are perfectly distinct from
each other. The mutual money would serve all the purposes of the
internal trade, leaving the hard money, and paper based on hard
money, to serve exclusively for the purposes of trade that reaches
out of the town. The mutual money will not prevent a single dollar of hard money, or paper based on hard money, from coming
into the town; for such hard money comes into the town, not in
consequence of exchanges made between the inhabitants themselves, but in consequence of produce sold abroad.* So long as
produce is sold out of the town, so long will the inhabitants be able
to buy commodities that are produced out of the town; and they

---

*These remarks may be generalized, and applied to the commerce
which is carried on between nations.

will be able to make purchases to the precise extent that they are
able to make sales. The mutual money will therefore prove to
them an unmixed benefit; it will be entirely independent of the old
money, and will open to them a new trade entirely independent of
the old trade. So far as it can be made available, it will unques-
tionably prove itself to be a good thing; and, where it cannot be
made available, the inhabitants will only be deprived of a benefit
that they could not have enjoyed—mutual money or no mutual
money. Besides, the comparative cost of the mutual money is almost nothing; for it can be issued to any amount on good security,
at the mere cost of printing, and the expense of looking after the
safety of the mortgages. If the mutual money should happen, at
any particular time, not to be issued to any great extent, it would
not be as though an immense mass of value was remaining idle; for
interest on the mutual money is precisely 0. The mutual money is
not itself actual value, but a mere medium for the exchange of actual values—a mere medium for the facilitation of barter.

We have remarked, that when the trader, who does the out-of-
town business of the inhabitants, buys coffee, sugar, etc., he does
not pay cash for them, but buys them at, say, six months' credit.
Now, the existing system of credit causes, by its very nature, periodical crises in commercial affairs. When one of these crises oc-
curs, the trader will say to the city merchant, "I owe you so much
for groceries; but 1 have no money, for times are hard: I will give
you, however, my note for the debt. Now, we leave it to the reader,
would not the city merchant prefer to take the mutual money of
the town to which the trader belongs, money that holds real estate
and produce in that town, rather than the private note of a trader
who may fail within a week?

If, under the existing system, all transactions were settled on
the spot in cash, things might be different, but as almost all transactions are conducted on the credit system, and as the credit system
necessarily involves periodical commercial crises, the mutual
money will find very little difficulty in ultimately forcing itself into
general circulation. The Mutual Bank is like the stone cut from
the mountain without hands, for let it be once established in a single village, no matter how obscure, and it will grow till it covers
the whole earth. Nevertheless, it would be better to obviate all
difficulty by starting the Mutual Bank on a sufficiently extensive
scale at the very beginning.

THE MEASURE OF VALUE.

The bill of a Mutual Bank is not a standard of value, since it
is itself measured and determined in value by the silver dollar. If
the dollar rises in value, the bill of the Mutual Bank rises also,
since it is receivable in lieu of a silver dollar. The bills of a Mutual
Bank are not standards of value, but mere instruments of exchange;
and as the value of mutual money is determined, not by the demand
and supply of mutual money, but by the demand and supply of the

precious metals, the Mutual Bank may issue bills to any extent, and those bills will not be liable to any depreciation from excess of supply And, for like reasons, mutual money will not be liable to rise in value if it happens at any time to be scarce in the market. The issues of mutual money are therefore susceptible of any contraction or expansion which may be necessary to meet the wants of the community, and such contraction or expansion cannot by any possibility be attended with any evil consequence whatever: for the silver dollar, which is the standard of value, will remain throughout at the natural valuation determined for it by the general demand and supply of gold and silver throughout the whole world.

The bills of Mutual Banks act merely as a medium of exchange they do not and cannot pretend to be measures or standards of value The medium of exchange is one thing; the measure of value is another, and the standard of value still another The dollar is the measure of value Silver and gold, at a certain degree of fineness, are the standard of value. The bill of a Mutual Bank is a bill of exchange, drawn by all the members of the mutual banking company upon themselves, indorsed and accepted by themselves, payable at sight, but only in services and products The members of the company bind themselves to receive their own money at par; that is, in lieu of as many silver dollars as are denoted by the denomination on the face of the bill Services and products are to be estimated in dollars, and exchanged for each other without the intervention of specie *

Mutual money, which neither is nor can be merchandise, escapes the law of supply and demand, which is applicable to merchandise only.

THE REGULATOR OF VALUE

The utility of an article is one thing, its exchangeable value is another, and the cost of its production is still another But the amount of labor expended in production, though not the measure, is, in the long run, the regulator of value, for every new invention which abridges labor, and enables an individual or company to offer an increased supply of valuable articles in the market brings with it an increase of competition For, supposing that one dollar constitutes a fair day's wages, and that one man by a certain process can produce an article valued in the market at one

---

*"I now undertake to affirm positively, and without the least fear that I can be answered, what heretofore I have but suggested—that a paper issued by the government, with the simple promise to receive it in all its dues, leaving its creditors to take it or gold and silver at their option, would, to the extent that it would circulate, form a perfect paper-circulation, which could not be abused by the government; that it would be as steady and uniform in value as the metals themselves, and that, if by possibility, it should depreciate, the loss would fall, not on the people, but on the government itself," etc.—J C. CALHOUN: Speech in reply to Mr Webster on the Sub-Treasury Bill, March 22, 1838

dollar in half a day's labor, other men will take advantage of the same process, and undersell the first man,
in order to get possession of the market. Thus, by the effect
of competition, the price of the article will probably be ultimately
reduced to fifty cents. Labor is the true regulator of value, for
every laboring man who comes into competition with others increases the supply of the products of labor, and thus diminishes
their value, while at the same time, and because he is a living
man, he increases the demand for those products to precisely the
same extent, and thus restores the balance for the laborer must be
housed, clothed and subsisted by the products of his labor. Thus
the addition of a laboring man, or of any number of laboring men,
to the mass of producers, ought to have no effect either upon the
price of labor, or upon that of commodities; since, if the laborer by
his presence increases the productive power, he at the same time
increases the demand for consumption. We know that things do
not always fall out thus in practice; but the irregularity is explained by the fact that the laborer, who ought himself to have the
produce of his labor, or its equivalent in exchange, has, by the
present false organization of credit, his wages abstracted from him
Want and over-production arise sometimes from mistakes in the direction of labor, but generally from that false organization of
credit which now obtains throughout the civilized world   There is
a market price of commodities, depending on supply and demand,
and a natural price, depending on the cost of production; and the
market price is in a state of continual oscillation, being sometimes
above, and sometimes below, the natural price but in the long run,
the average of a series of years being taken, it coincides with it.   It
is probable that, under a true organization of credit, the natural
price and market price would coincide at every moment.* Under
the present system, there are no articles whose market and natural
prices coincide so nearly and so constantly as those of the precious
metals; and it is for this reason that they have been adopted by the
various nations as standards of value

When Adam Smith and Malthus† say that labor is a measure of

---

*The theory that the laborer should receive sufficient wages to buy
back his product, and thus prevent over-production, was discovered almost simultaneously by a number of writers about fifty years ago. The
value of this discovery to economics is as great as Newton's was to
physics, or Darwin's to biology.—EDITOR.

†Malthus says (we quote the substance, and very possibly the exact
words, though we have not the book by us): "If a man is born into a
world already occupied, and his family is not able to support him, or if
society has no demand for his labor, that man has no right to claim any
nourishment whatever, he is really one too many on the earth   At the
great banquet of nature there is no plate laid for him   Nature com-
mands him to take himself away; and she will by no means delay in
putting her own order into execution."

value, they speak, not of the labor which an article cost, or ought to have cost, in its production, but of the quantity of labor which the article may purchase or command. It is very well, for those who mistake the philosophy of speculation on human misfortune and necessities for social science, to assume for measure of value the amount of labor which different commodities can command Considered from this point of view, the price of commodities is regulated, not in the labor expended in their production, but by the distress and want of the laboring class There is no device of the political economists so infernal as the one which ranks labor as a commodity, varying in value according to supply and demand Neither is there any device so unphilosophical; since the ratio of the supply of labor to the demand for it is unvarying for every producer is also a consumer, and rightfully, to the precise extent of the amount of his products; the laborer who saves up his wages being, so far as society is concerned, and in the long run, a consumer of those wages. The supply and demand for labor is virtually unvarying, and its price ought, therefore, to be constant, Labor is said to be value, not because it is itself merchandise, but because of the values it contains, as it were, in solution, or, to use the correct metaphysical term, *in potentia* The value of labor is a figurative expression, and a fiction, like the productiveness of capital Labor, like liberty, love, ambition, genius, is something vague and indeterminate in its nature, and is rendered definite by its object only; misdirected labor produces no value Labor is said to be valuable, not because it can itself be valued, but because the products of labor may be truly valuable. When we say "John's labor is worth a dollar a day," it is as though we said, "The daily product of John's labor is worth a dollar." To speak of labor as merchandise is treason, for such speech denies the true dignity of man, who is the king of the earth Where labor is merchandise in fact (not by a mere inaccuracy of language) there man is merchandise also, whether it be in England or South Carolina

THE WAY IN WHICH THE AFFAIRS OF THE MUTUAL BANK MAY BE CLOSED

When the company votes to issue no more money, the bills it has already issued will be returned upon it; for, since the bills were issued in discounting notes running to maturity, the debtors of the bank, as their notes mature, will pay in the bills they have received When the debtors have paid their debts to the bank, then the bills are all in, every debtor has discharged his mortgage, and the affairs of the bank are closed. If any debtor fails to pay, the bank sells the property mortgaged, and pays itself. The bank lends at a rate of interest that covers its bare expenses: it makes, therefore, no profits, and, consequently, can declare no dividends It is by its nature incapable of owing anything: it has, therefore, no debts to settle When the bank's debtors have paid their debts to the bank, then nobody owes anything to the bank, and the bank owes nothing to anybody.

In case some of the debtors of the bank redeem their notes, not in bills of the Mutual Bank, but in bills of specie-paying banks, then those bills of specie-paying banks will be at once presented for redemption at the institutions that issued them; and an amount of specie will come into the hands of the Mutual Bank, precisely equal to the amount of its own bills still in circulation; for since the Mutual Bank never issues money, except in discounting notes running to maturity, the notes of the debtors to the bank precisely cover the amount of the bank's money in circulation. When this specie comes into the hands of the bank, it deposits it at once in some other institution; which institution assumes the responsibility of redeeming at sight such of the bills of the closed bank as may be at any time thereafter presented for redemption. And such institution will gladly assume this responsibility, since it is probable that many of the bills will be lost or destroyed, and therefore never presented for redemption; and such loss or destruction will be a clear gain to the institution assuming the responsibility, since it has specie turned over to it for the redemption of every one of the bills that remains out.

Finally: let us conceive, for a moment, of the manifold imperfections of the existing system of banking. In Massachusetts, the banks had out, in the year 1849, nine and one-half dollars of paper* for every one dollar of specie in their vaults wherewith to redeem them. Can any thing be more absurd than the solemn promise made by the banks to redeem nine and one-half paper-dollars with one dollar in specie? They may get along very well with this promise in a time of profound calm; but what would they do on occasions of panic?†

The paper issued under the existing system is an article of merchandise, varying in price with the variations of supply and demand: it is, therefore, unfit to serve as a medium of exchange.

The banks depend on the merchants; so that, when the merchant is poor, it falls out that the bank is always still poorer. Of what use is the bank, if it calls in its issues in hard times—the very occasions when increased issues are demanded by the wants of the community?

The existing bank reproduces the aristocratic organizations; it has its Spartan element of privileged stockholders, its Laconian element of obsequious speculators, and, on the outside, a multitude of Helots who are excluded from its advantages   Answer us, read-

---

*Counting, of course, the certificates of deposit which are convertible into specie on demand.

†Notwithstanding the fact that this work was written in criticism of the banking system in vogue in 1850, most people persist in calling it a "revival of the old wild-cat banks that existed before the war."—EDITOR

er: If we are able, at this time, to bring forward the existing banking system as a new thing, and should recommend its adoption, would you not laugh in our face, and characterize our proposition as ridiculous? Yet the existing system has an actual and practical being, in spite of all its imperfections. nay, more, it is the ruling element of the present civilization of the Christian world; it has substituted itself, or is now substituting itself, in the place of monarchies and nobilities. Who is the noble of the present day, if not the man who lends money at interest? Who is the emperor, if not Pereire or Baron Rothschild? Now, if the present system of banking is capable of actual existence, how much more capable of actual existence is the system of mutual banking! Mutual banking combines all the good elements of the method now in operation, and is capable of securing a thousand benefits which the present method cannot compass, and is, moreover, free from all its disadvantages!

CHAPTER VI.

THE PROVINCIAL LAND BANK.*

"In the year 1714," says Governor Hutchinson, in his "History of Massachusetts," a certain "party had projected a private bank; or, rather, had taken up a project published in London in the year 1684; but this not being generally known in America, a merchant of Boston was the reputed father of it. There was nothing more in it than issuing bills of credit, which all the members of the company promised to receive as money, but at no certain value compared with silver and gold; and real estate to a sufficient value were to be bound as a security that the company should perform their engagements. They were soliciting the sanction of the General Court, and an act of government to incorporate them. This party generally consisted of persons in difficult or involved circumstances in trade; or such as were possessed of real estates; but had little or no ready money at command; or men of no substance at all; and we may well enough suppose the party to be very numerous. Some, no doubt, joined them from mistaken principles, and an apprehension that it was a scheme beneficial to the public; and some for party's sake and public applause.

"Three of the representatives from Boston—Mr. Cooke; Mr Noyes, a gentlemen in great esteem with the inhabitants in general; and Mr Payne—were the supporters of the party. Mr. Hutchinson, the other (an attempt to leave him out of the House not succeeding), was sent from the House to the Council, where his opposition would be of less consequence. The governor was no favorer of the scheme; but the lieutenant-governor—a gentleman of no great fortune, and whose stipend from the government was trifling—engaged in the cause with great zeal.

"A third party, though very opposite to the private bank, yet were no enemies to bills of credit. They were in favor of loan-bills from the government to any of the inhabitants who would mortgage their estates as a security for the repayment of the bills with interest in a term of years: the interest to be paid annually, and applied to the support of government. This was an easy way of paying public charges; which, no doubt, they wondered that in so many ages the wisdom of other governments had never discovered. The principal men of the Council were in favor of it; and, it being thought by the first

---

*It is worthy of note that the present-day historians, who take such pains to show their intimate knowledge of the financial plans of remote times, studiously avoid mentioning this one —Editor.

party the least of two evils, they fell in with the scheme; and, after that, the country was divided between the public and private bank The House of Representatives was nearly equally divided, but rather favorers of the private bank, from the great influence of the Boston members in the House, and a great number of persons of the town out of it. The controversy had a universal spread, and divided towns, parishes, and particular families.

"At length, after a long struggle, the party for the public bank prevailed in the General Court for a loan of £50,000 in bills of credit, which were put into the hands of trustees, and let for five years only, to any of the inhabitants, at 5 per cent interest, one-fifth part of the principal to be paid annually. This lessened the number of the party for the private bank; but it increased the zeal, and raised a strong resentment, in those that remained."—(Thomas Hutchinson: "History of Massachusetts," vol. ii., p 188).

It is utterly inconceivable that any company of sane men should have seriously proposed to issue paper money destitute of all fixed and determinate value as compared with gold and silver, imagining that such money would circulate as currency If paper money has "no certain value compared with silver and gold," it has no certain value compared with any commodity whatever, that is, it has no certain value at all: for, since gold and silver have a determinate value as compared with exchangeable commodities, all paper money that may be estimated in terms of marketable commodities, may be estimated in terms of silver and gold. Our author will permit us to suspect that his uncompromising hostility, not only to the land-bank, but also to everything else of a democratic tendency, blinded his eyes to the true nature of the institution he describes Our suspicion is strengthened when we read that the paper money in question was to have a determinate value, since it was to have been secured by a pledge of "real estate to a sufficient value." The projectors of the scheme probably intended that the members of the company should redeem their bills from the bill-holders by receiving them, in all payments, in lieu of determinate and specified amounts of gold and silver; and such a method of redemption would have given the bills "a certain value as compared with silver and gold "*

In view of this extract from Governor Hutchinson's history, we

---

*"North Carolina, just after the Revolution, issued a large amount of paper, which was made receivable in dues to her It was also made a legal tender, which, of course, was not obligatory after the adoption of the Federal Constitution A large amount, say between four and five hundred thousand dollars, remained in circulation after that period, and continued to circulate for more than twenty years, at par with gold and silver during the whole time, with no other advantage than being received in the revenue of the State, which was much less than one hundred thousand dollars per annum "—JOHN C. CALHOUN Speech on the bill authorizing an issue of treasury notes, Sept 19, 1837

abandon all claims to novelty or originality as regards our own
scheme for a Mutual Bank. We think it very probable that our
theory dates back to "the project published in London in the year
1684." but we affirm nothing positively on this head, since we are
altogether ignorant of the details, not only of the provincial project,
but also of the original London plan. We have no information in
regard to these matters, except that which is now submitted to the
reader.

Our author says, on a subsequent page:

"In 1739, a great part of the Province was disposed to favor
what was called the land bank or manufactory scheme; which was
begun, or rather revived, in this year, and produced such great and
lasting mischiefs, that a particular relation of the rise, progress
and overthrow of it may be of use to discourage any attempts of the
like nature in future ages."—("History of Massachusetts," vol. ii.,
352).

It appears that after an interval of twenty-five years, the land-
bank scheme rose once again above the surface of the political and
financial waters. Governor Hutchinson says that this scheme produced "great and lasting mischiefs." Let us see what these "mischiefs" were:

"The project of the bank of 1714 was revived. The projector of
that bank now put himself at the head of seven or eight hundred
persons, some few of rank and good estate, but generally of low
condition among the plebeians, and of small estate, and many of
them perhaps insolvent. This notable company were to give credit
to £150,000 lawful money, to be issued in bills; each person to mortgage a real estate in proportion to the sums he subscribed and took
out, or to give bond with two sureties: but personal security was
not to be taken for more than £100 from any one person. Ten directors and a treasurer were to be chosen by the company. Every
subscriber or partner was to pay 3 per cent interest [per annum]
for the sum taken out, and 5 per cent of the principal;* and he that
did not pay bills might pay the produce and manufacture of the
Province at such rates as the directors from time to time should
set: and they [the bills] should commonly pass in lawful money.
The pretence was, that, by thus furnishing a medium and instrument of trade, not only the inhabitants in general would be better
able to procure the Province bills of credit for their taxes, but
trade, foreign and inland, would revive and flourish, The fate of
the project was thought to depend on the opinion which the General Court should form of it. It was necessary, therefore, to have a
house of representatives well disposed. Besides the 800 persons
subscribers, the needy part of the Province in general favored the
scheme. One of their votes will go as far in elections as one of the
most opulent. The former are most numerous, and it appeared

---

*Thus the whole principal would be paid up in twenty years.

that by far the majority of representatives for 1740 were subscribers to or favorers of the scheme, and they have ever since been distinguished by the name of the Land-Bank House.

"Men of estates and the principal merchants of the Province abhorred the project, and refused to receive the bills; but great numbers of shop-keepers who had lived for a long time on the fraud of a depreciating currency, and many small traders, gave credit to the bills. The directors, it was said, by a vote of the company, became traders,* and issued just such bills as they thought proper, without any fund or security for their ever being redeemed. They purchased every sort of commodity, ever so much a drug, for the sake of pushing off their bills; and, by one means or other, a large sum—perhaps fifty or sixty thousand pounds—was floated. To lessen the temptation to receive the bills, a company of merchants agreed to issue their notes, or bills, redeemable in silver and gold at distant periods, much like the scheme in 1733, and attended with no better effect. The governor exerted himself to blast this fraudulent undertaking—the land-bank. Not only such civil and military officers as were directors or partners, but all who received or paid any of the bills were displaced. The governor negatived the person chosen speaker of the House, being a director of the bank; and afterwards negatived thirteen of the newly elected counsellors, who were directors or partners in, or favorers of, the scheme. But all was insufficient to suppress it. Perhaps the major part in number of the inhabitants of the Province openly or secretly, were well-wishers of it. One of the directors afterwards acknowledged to me that, although he entered into the company with a view to the public interest, yet, when he found what power and influence they had in all public concerns, he was convinced it was more than belonged to them, more than they could make a good use of, and therefore unwarrantable. Many of the more sensible, discreet persons of the Province saw a general confusion at hand. The authority of the Parliament to control all public and private persons and proceedings in the Colonies, was at that day questioned by nobody. Application was therefore made to Parliament for an act to suppress the company; which, notwithstanding the opposition made by their agent, was very easily obtained, and therein it was declared that the act of the Sixth of King George I., chapter xviii., did, does and shall extend to the colonies and plantations of America. It was said the act of George I., when it was passed, had no relation to America; but another act, twenty years after, gave it force, even from the passing it, which it never could have had without. This was said to be an instance of the transcendent power of Parliament. Although the company was dissolved, yet the act of Parliament gave the possessors of the bills a right of action against every

*See foregoing paragraph where it is said that debts to the bank might be paid in manufactures and produce.

partner or director for the sums expressed, WITH INTEREST The
company was in a maze At a general meeting, some, it is said,
were for running all hazards, although the act subjected them to a
præmunire; but the directors had more prudence, and advised them
to declare that they considered themselves dissolved, and meet only
to consult upon some method of redeeming their bills of the possessors, which every man engaged to endeavor in proportion to his interest, and to pay in to the directors, or some of them, to burn or
destroy. Had the company issued their bills at the value expressed
on the face of them, they would have had no reason to complain at
being obliged to redeem them at the same rate, but as this was not
the case in general, and many of the possessors of the bills had acquired them for half their value, as expressed equity could not
be done; and, so far as respected the company, perhaps, the Parliament was not very anxious; the loss they sustained being but a just
penalty for their unwarrantable undertaking, if it had been properly applied. Had not the Parliament interposed, the Province
would have been in the utmost confusion, and the authority of
government entirely in the Land-Bank Company."—(p. 353.)

The "mischiefs" occasioned by this land-bank seems to have
been political, rather than economical, for our author nowhere
affirms that the bill holders, not members of the company lost anything by the institution. We would remark that there are certain
"mischiefs" which are regarded not without indulgence by poster-
ity. Governor Hutchinson ought to have explained more in detail
the nature of the evils he complains of; and also to have told us
why he, a declared enemy of popular institutions, opposed the advocates of the bank so uncompromisingly. Mutualism operates, by
its very nature, to render political government founded on arbitrary force, superfluous; that is, it operates to the decentralization
of the political power, and to the transformation of the state, by
substituting self-government in the stead of government *ab extra* *
The Land-Bank of 1740, which embodied the mutual principle, op-
erated vigorously in opposition to the government. Can we wonder
that it had to be killed by an arbitrary stretch "of the supreme
power of Parliament," and by an *ex post facto* law bearing
outrageously on the individual members of the company? For our
part, we admire the energy—the confidence in the principle of mutualism—of those members who proposed to go on in spite of
Parliament, "although the act subjected them to a *præmunire.*"
If they had gone on, they would simply have anticipated the American Revolution by some thirty years.

But where is the warning to future ages? According to Governor Hutchinson's own statement, the fault of the bank was, that
it would have succeeded TOO WELL if it had had a fair trial; nay,

---

*This is also Proudhon's theory; which he felicitously called "the
dissolution of government in the economic organism."—EDITOR.

that it would have succeeded in spite of all obstacles had it not been for the exertion of "the transcendent power of Parliament." Where is the bank of these degenerate days that has shown anything like the same power of endurance? Some of the existing banks find it difficult to live with the power of government exerted in their favor!

The attempt of the Land-Bank Company to republicanize gold and silver, and to make all commodities circulate as ready money was, without question, premature. But our author misapprehends the matter, mistaking a transformation of the circulating medium for a mercantile scheme. The "vote of the company whereby the directors became traders," was an act for transforming the currency. We do not justify it altogether; for it put the welfare of the cause at too great hazard; but it was, nevertheless, not totally out of harmony with the general system. We remark in conclusion, that the depreciation in the provincial currency was occasioned, not by "land-bank," that is, by mutual paper—which the Parliament forced the issuers, by an arbitrary, vindictive, and tyrannical law, to redeem WITH INTEREST—but it was occasioned by government paper, "professing to be ultimately redeemable in gold and silver."[*] All arguments, therefore, against mutual money, derived from the colonial currency, are foreign to the purpose.

The main objections against mutual banking are as follows: 1. It is a novelty, and therefore a chimera of the inventor's brain; 2. It is an old story, borrowed from provincial history, and therefore of no account!

How would you have us answer objections like these? Things new or old may be either good or evil. Every financial scheme should stand or fall by its own intrinsic merits, and not be judged from extraneous considerations.

---

[*] "We are told that there is no instance of a government paper that did not depreciate. In reply I affirm that there is none assuming the form I propose (notes receivable by government in payment of dues) that ever did depreciate. Whenever a paper receivable in the dues of government had anything like a fair trial, it has succeeded. Instance the case of North Carolina referred to in my opening remarks. The drafts of the treasury at this moment, with all their incumbrance, are nearly at par with gold and silver; and I might add the instance alluded to by the distinguished senator from Kentucky, in which he admits, that as soon as the excess of the issues of the Commonwealth Bank of Kentucky were reduced to the proper point, its notes rose to par. The case of Russia might also be mentioned. In 1827 she had a fixed paper-circulation in the form of bank-notes, but which were inconvertible, of upward of $120,000,000, estimated in the metallic ruble, and which had for years remained without fluctuation; having nothing to sustain it but that it was received in the dues of government, and that, too, with a revenue of only about $90,000,000 annually."—JOHN C. CALHOUN: Speech on his amendment to separate the government from the banks, Oct. 3, 1837

CHAPTER VII.

MONEY.

The most concise and expressive definition of the term "capital," which we have seen in the writings of the political economists, is the one furnished by J. Stuart Mill, in his table of contents. He says: "Capital is wealth appropriated to reproductive employment." There is, indeed, a certain ambiguity attached to the word wealth; but let that pass; we accept the definition. A tailor has $5 in money, which he proposes to employ in his business. This money is unquestionably capital, since it is wealth appropriated to reproductive employment: but it may be expended in the purchase of cloth, in the payment of journeymen's wages, or in a hundred other ways; what kind of capital, then, is it? It is evidently, disengaged capital. Let us say that the tailor takes his money and expends it for cloth; this cloth is also devoted to reproductive employment, and is therefore still capital; but what kind of capital? Evidently, engaged capital. He makes this cloth into a coat; which coat is more valuable than the cloth, since it is the result of human labor bestowed upon the cloth. But the coat is no longer capital; for it is no longer (so far, at least, as the occupation of the tailor is concerned), capable of being appropriated to reproductive employment; what is it, then? It is that for the creation of which the capital was originally appropriated; it is product. The tailor takes this coat and sells it in the market for $8; which dollars become to him a new disengaged capital. The circle is complete; the coat becomes engaged capital to the purchaser; and the money is disengaged capital, with which the tailor may commence another operation. Money is disengaged capital, and disengaged capital is money. Capital passes, therefore, through various forms; first it is disengaged capital, then it becomes engaged capital, then it becomes product, afterwards it is transformed again into disengaged capital, thus recommencing its circular progress.

The community is happy and prosperous when all professions of men easily exchange with each other the products of their labor; that is, the community is happy and prosperous when money circulates freely, and each man is able with facility to transform his product into disengaged capital, for with disengaged capital, or money, men may command such of the products of labor as they desire, to the extent, at least, of the purchasing power of their money.

The community is unhappy, unprosperous, miserable, when money is scarce, when exchanges are effected with difficulty. For notice, that, in the present state of the world, there is never real over-production to any appreciable extent; for, whenever the baker

has too much bread, there are always laborers who could produce
that of which the baker has too little, and who are themselves in
want of bread. It is when the tailor and baker cannot exchange,
that there is want and over-production on both sides. Whatever,
therefore, has power to withdraw the currency from circulation,
has power, also, to cause trade to stagnate; power to overwhelm
the community with misery; power to carry want, and its correla-
tive, over-production, into every artisan's house and workshop.
For the transformation of product into disengaged capital, is one of
the regular steps of production; and whatever withdraws the disengaged capital, or money, from circulation, at once renders this
step impossible, and thus puts a drag on all production.

THERE ARE VARIOUS KINDS OF MONEY.

But all money is not the same money. There is one money of
gold, another of silver, another of brass, another of leather, and
another of paper and there is a difference in the glory of these
different kinds of money. There is one money that is a commodity,
having its exchangeable value determined by the law of supply and
demand, which money may be called (though somewhat barbarous-
ly) merchandise-money; as for instance, gold, silver, brass, bank-
bills, etc ; there is another money, which is not a commodity,
whose exchangeable value is altogether independent of the law of
supply and demand, and which may be called mutual money

Mr. Edward Kellogg says: "Money becomes worthless whenever it ceases to be capable of accumulating an income which can
be exchanged for articles of actual value. The value of money as
much depends upon its power of being loaned for an income, as the
value of a farm depends upon its natural power to produce." And
again. "Money is valuable in proportion to its power to accumulate value by interest."* Mr. Kellogg is mistaken. Money
is a commodity in a twofold way, and has therefore a twofold value and a twofold price—one value as an article that can be exchanged for other commodities, and another value as an article
that can be loaned out at interest, one price which is determined
by the supply and demand of the precious metals, and another
price (the rate of interest) which is determined by the distress of
the borrowing community. Mr. Kellogg speaks as though this last
value and last price were the only ones deserving consideration;
but this is by no means the case; for this last value and price are so
far from being essential to the nature of money, that the Mutual
Bank will one day utterly abolish them. The natural value of the
silver dollar depends upon the demand and supply of the metal of
which it is composed and not upon its artificial power to accumulate value by interest. Legislation has created usury; and the

---

*People who raise the cry of "cheap money" fall into the same error,
money that circulates freely at par, whether interest-bearing or not, is
neither cheap or dear.—EDITOR.

Mutual Bank can destroy it. Usury is a result of the legislation which establishes a particular commodity as the sole article of legal tender; and, when all commodities are made to be ready money through the operation of mutual banking, usury will vanish.

CONVERTIBLE PAPER-MONEY RENDERS THE STANDARD OF VALUE UNCERTAIN.

To show the effect of variations in the volume of the existing circulating medium, not only on foreign commerce, but also on the private interests of each individual member of the community, we will, at the risk of being tedious, have recourse to an illustration. Let us suppose that the whole number of dollars (either in specie or convertible paper) in circulation, at a particular time, is equal to Y; and that the sum of all these dollars will buy a certain determinate quantity of land, means of transportation, merchandise, etc., which may be represented by x; for, if money may be taken as the measure and standard of value for commodities, then conversely, commodities may be taken as the standard and measure of value for money. Let us say, therefore, that the whole mass of the circulating medium is equal to Y; and that its value, estimated in terms of land, ships, houses, merchandise, etc., is equal to x If, now, the quantity of specie and convertible paper we have supposed to be in circulation be suddenly doubled, so that the whole mass becomes equal in volume to 2Y, the value of the whole mass will undergo no change, but will still be equal to x, neither more nor less. This is truly wonderful! Some young mathematician, fresh from his algebra, will hasten to contradict us, and say that the value of the whole mass will be equal to $2x$, or perhaps to x divided by 2, but it is the young mathematician who is in error, as may easily be made manifest The multiplication of the whole number of dollars by 2 causes money to be twice as easy to be obtained as it was before. Such multiplication causes, therefore, each individual dollar to fall to one-half its former value; and this for the simple reason that the price of silver dollars, or their equivalents in convertible paper, depends upon the ratio of the supply of such dollars to the demand for them, and that every increase in the supply causes therefore a proportionate decrease in the price. The variation in the volume does not cause a variation in the value of the volume, but causes a variation in the price of the individual dollar. Again, if one-half the money in circulation be suddenly withdrawn, so that the whole volume shall equal ½Y, the value of the new volume will be exactly equal to x, for the reason that the difficulty in procuring money will be doubled, since the supply will be diminished one-half, causing each individual dollar to rise to double its former value. The value of the whole mass in circulation is independent of the variations of the volume, for every increase in the volume causes a proportionate decrease in the value of the individual dollar, and every decrease in the volume causes proportionate increase in the value of the individual dollar. If the mass of our existing circulating medium were increased a hundred-fold, the multiplication would have no effect other than that of reducing the value of the individual dollar to that of the existing individual cent. If gold were as plenty as iron, it would command no higher price than iron If our money were composed of iron, we should be obliged to hire an ox-cart for the transportation of $100; and it would be as difficult, under such conditions, to obtain a cart-load of iron, as it is now to obtain its value in our present currency.

A fall or rise in the price of money, and a rise or fall in the price of all other commodities besides money, are precisely the same economical phenomenon.

The effect of a change in the volume of the currency is therefore not a change in the value of the whole volume, but a change in the value of the individual silver dollar, this change being indicated by a variation in the price of commodities; a fall in the price of the silver dollar being indicated by a rise in the price of commodities, and a rise in the price of the dollar being indicated by a fall in the price of commodities. "The value of money," says J. Stuart Mill, other things being the same, "varies inversely as its quantity; every increase of quantity lowering its value, and every diminution raising it in a ratio exactly equivalent. That an increase of the quantity of money raises prices, and a diminution lowers them, is the most elementary proposition in the theory of the currency, and, without it, we should have no key to any of the others."

Let us use this key for the purpose of unlocking the practical mysteries attached to variations in the volume of the existing currency. The banks, since they exercise control over the volume of the currency by means of the power they possess of increasing or diminishing, at pleasure, the amount of paper money in circulation, exercise control also over the value of every individual dollar in every private man's pocket. They make great issues, and money becomes plenty; that is to say, every other commodity becomes dear. The capitalist sells what he has to sell while prices are high. The banks draw in their issues, and money becomes scarce; that is, all other commodities become cheap The community is distressed for money. Individuals are forced to sell property to raise money to pay their debts, and to sell at a loss on account of the state of the market. Then the capitalist buys what he desires to buy while prices are low. These operations are the upper and the nether mill-stones, between which the hopes of the people are ground to powder

THE EVILS OF CONVERTIBLE PAPER MONEY.

Paper professing to be convertible into silver and gold, by over-stocking the home-market with money, makes specie to be in less demand in this country than it is abroad, and renders profitable an undue exportation of gold and silver; thus occasioning a chronic drain of the precious metals.*

*Persons of little foresight rejoice in the high price of commodi-

It increases the volume of the currency, and therefore decreases the value of the individual silver dollar; thus causing an enhancement in the price of all domestic commodities; giving an unnatural advantage in our own markets to foreign manufacturers, who live in the enjoyment of a more valuable currency and presenting irresistible inducements to our own merchants to purchase abroad rather than at home.

It operates to give control over the currency to certain organized bodies of men, enabling them to exercise partiality, and loan capital to their relatives and favorites; thus encouraging incapacity, and depressing merit; and therefore demoralizing the people who are led to believe that legitimate business, which should be founded altogether upon capital, industry and talent, partakes of the nature of court-favor and gambling.

It operates to encourage unwise speculation; and, by furnishing artificial facilities to rash, scheming and incompetent persons, induces the burying of immense masses of capital in unremunerative enterprises.

It reduces the value of our own currency below the level of the value of money throughout the world, rendering over-importation inevitable, causing our markets to be overstocked with foreign goods, and thus making the ordinary production of the country to present all the calamitous effects of over-production.

It operates inevitably to involve the country and individuals doing business in the country, in foreign debts. It operates also, by blinding the people to the true nature of money, and encouraging them to raise funds for the commencement and completion of hazardous enterprises by the sale of scrip and bonds abroad, to mortgage the country, and the produce of its industry, to foreign holders of obligations against us, etc.

ADVANTAGES OF A MUTUAL CURRENCY.

Mutual Banks would furnish an adequate currency; for whether money were hard or easy, all legitimate paper would be discounted by them. At present, banks draw in their issues when money is scarce (the very time when a large issue is desirable), because they are afraid there will be a run upon them for specie; but Mutual Banks, having no fear of a run upon them—as they have no metallic capital, and never pretend to pay specie for their bills—can always discount good paper.

It may appear to some readers, notwithstanding the explana-

---

ties—that is, in the low price or plentifulness of money—not reflecting that, when money is too plenty, the sap and vitality of the country flow forth in a constant stream to enrich foreign lands. An excessive supply of money causes a deceitful appearance of prosperity, and favors temporarily a few manufacturers, traders and mechanics; but it is always a source of unnumbered calamities to the whole country.

tions already given*, that we go altogether farther than we are
warranted when we affirm that the creation of an immense mass of
mutual money would produce no depreciation in the price of the silver dollar. The difficulty experienced in understanding this matter
results from incorrect notions respecting the standard of value, the
measure of value, and the nature of money. This may be made
evident by illustration. The yard is a measure of length; and a
piece of wood, or a rod of glass or metal, is a corresponding standard of length The yard, or measure, being ideal, is unvarying; but
all the standards we have mentioned contract or expand by heat or
cold, so that they vary (to an almost imperceptible degree, perhaps)
at every moment. It is almost impossible to measure off a yard, or
any other given length, with mathematical accuracy. The measure of value is the dollar; the standard of value, as fixed by law, is
silver or gold at a certain degree of fineness Corn, land, or any
other merchantable commodity might serve as a standard of value,
but silver and gold form a more perfect standard, on account of
their being less liable to variation; and they have accordingly been
adopted, by the common consent of all nations, to serve as such.
The dollar, as simple measure of value, has—like the yard, which is
a measure of length—an ideal existence only. In Naples, the ducat
is the measure of value; but the Neapolitans have no specific coin
of that denomination. Now, it is evident that the bill of a Mutual
Bank is like a note of hand, or like an ordinary bank bill, neither a
measure, nor a standard of value. It is (1) not a measure; for, un-
like all measures, it has an actual, and not a merely ideal existence.
The bill of a Mutual Bank, being receivable in lieu of a specified
number of silver dollars presupposes the existence of the silver dollar as measure of value, and acknowledges itself as amenable to
that measure The silver dollar differs from a bill of a Mutual
Bank receivable in lieu of a silver dollar, as the measure differs
from the thing measured. The bill of a Mutual Bank is (2) not a
standard of value, because it has in itself no intrinsic value, like
silver and gold; its value being legal, and not actual. A stick has
actual length, and therefore may serve as a standard of length;
silver has actual intrinsic value, and may therefore serve as a
standard of value; but the bill of a Mutual Bank, having a legal
value only, and not an actual one, cannot serve as a standard of
value, but is referred, on the contrary, to silver and gold as that
standard, without which it would itself be utterly unintelligible.

If ordinary bank bills represented specie actually existing in
the vaults of the banks, no mere issue or withdrawal of them
could effect a fall or rise in the value of money; for every issue of a
dollar-bill would correspond to the locking up of a specie dollar in

*Perhaps on account of those explanations. As heat melts wax, and
hardens clay, so the same general principles, as applied to merchandise
money and to mutual money, give opposite results

the bank's vaults; and every cancelling of a dollar-bill would correspond to the issue by the banks of a specie dollar. It is by the exercise of banking privileges—that is, by the issue of bills purporting to be, but which are not, convertible—that the banks effect a depreciation in the price of the silver dollar. It is this fiction (by which legal value is assimilated to, and becomes, to all business intents and purposes, actual value) that enables bank-notes to depreciate the silver dollar. Substitute verity in the place of fiction, either by permitting the banks to issue no more paper than they have specie in their vaults, or by effecting an entire divorce between bank-paper and its pretended specie basis, and the power of paper to depreciate specie is at an end. So long as the fiction is kept up, the silver dollar is depreciated, and tends to emigrate for the purpose of traveling in foreign parts; but the moment the fiction is destroyed, the power of paper over metal ceases. By its intrinsic nature specie is merchandise, having its value determined, as such, by supply and demand; but on the contrary, paper-money is, by its intrinsic nature, not merchandise, but the means whereby merchandise is exchanged, and as such ought always to be commensurate in quantity with the amount of merchandise to be exchanged, be that amount great or small. Mutual money is measured by specie, but is in no way assimilated to it; and therefore its issue can have no effect whatever to cause a rise or fall in the price of the precious metals.

CHAPTER VIII.

CREDIT.

We are obliged to make a supposition by no means flattering to the individual presented to the reader. Let us suppose, therefore, that some miserable mortal, who is utterly devoid of any personal good quality to recommend him, makes his advent on the stage of action, and demands credit. Are there circumstances under which he can obtain it? Most certainly. Though he possesses neither energy, morality nor business capacity, yet if he owns a farm worth $2,000, which he is willing to mortgage as security for $1,500 that he desires to borrow, he will be considered as eminently deserving of credit. He is neither industrious, punctual, capable, nor virtuous; but he owns a farm clear of debt worth $2,000 and verily he shall raise the $1,500!

Personal credit is one thing; real credit is another and a very different thing. In one case, it is the man who receives credit, in the other, it is the property, the thing. Personal credit is in the nature of partnership; real credit is in the nature of a sale, with a reserved right of repurchase under conditions. By personal credit, two men or more are brought into voluntary mutual relations; by real credit, a certain amount of fixed property is transformed, under certain conditions and for a certain time, into circulating medium; that is, a certain amount of engaged capital is temporarily transformed into disengaged capital.

THE USURY LAWS.

We have already spoken of the absurdity of the usury laws. But let that pass; we will speak of it again.

A young man goes to a capitalist, saying: "If you will lend me $100, I will go into a certain business, and make $1,500 in the course of the present year, and my profits will thus enable me to pay you back the money you lend me, and another $100 for the use of it. Indeed it is nothing more than fair that I should pay you as much as I offer; for, after all, there is a great risk in the business, and you do me a greater favor than I do you." The capitalist answers: "I cannot lend you money on such terms; for the transaction would be illegal; nevertheless, I am willing to help you all I can, if I can devise a way. What do you say to my buying such rooms and machinery as you require, and letting them to you on the terms you propose? For, though I cannot charge more than 6 per cent on money loaned, I can let buildings, whose total value is only $100, at a rate of $100 per annum, and violate no law. Or, again, as I shall be obliged to furnish you with the raw material consumed in your business, what do you say to our entering into a partnership, so arranging the terms of agreement that the profits will be divided in fact, as they would be in the case that I loaned you $100 at 100 per cent interest per annum?" The young man will probably permit the capitalist to arrange the transaction in any form he pleases, provided the money is actually forthcoming. If the usury laws speak any intelligible language to the capitalist, it is this: "The legislature does not intend that you shall lend money to any young man to help in his business, where the insurance upon the money you trust in his hands, and which is subjected to the risk of his transactions, amounts to more than 6 per cent per annum on the amount loaned." And, in this speech, the deep wisdom of the legislature is manifested! Why six, rather than five or seven? Why any restriction at all?

Now for the other side (for we have thus far spoken of the usury laws as they bear on mere personal credit): If a man borrows $1,500 on the mortgage of a farm, worth, in the estimation of the creditor himself, $2,000, why should he pay 6 per cent interest on the money borrowed? What does this interest cover? Insurance? Not at all; for the money is perfectly safe, as the security given is confessedly ample; the insurance is 0. Does the interest cover the damage which the creditor suffers by being kept out of his money for the time specified in the contract? This cannot be the fact—for the damage is also 0—since a man who lends out money at interest, on perfect security, counts the total amount of interest as clear gain, and would much prefer letting the money at ¼ per cent to permitting it to remain idle. The rate of interest upon money lent on perfect security is commensurate, not with the risk the creditor runs of losing his money—for that risk is 0; not to the inconvenience to which the creditor is put by letting the money go out of his hands—for that inconvenience is also 0,* since the creditor lends only such money as he himself does not wish to use; but it is commensurate with the distress of the borrower. One per cent per annum interest on money lent on perfect security is, therefore, too high a rate; and all levying of interest-money on perfect security is profoundedly immoral,† since such interest-money is the fruit of the speculation of one man upon the misfortune of another. Yet the legislature permits one citizen to speculate upon the misfortune of another to the amount of six-hundredths per annum of the extent to which he gets him into his power! This is the morality of the usury laws in their bearing on real credit.

---

*If, however, the inconvenience is anything, the lender ought to be indemnified; but such indemnification is not properly interest.

†Perhaps, we ought rather to say, "would be profoundly immoral in a more perfect social order." We suppose that must be considered right, in our present chaotic state, which is best on the whole, or which—taking men's passion as they are—is unavoidable.

LEGITIMATE CREDIT.

All the questions connected with credit, the usury laws, etc , may be forever set at rest by the establishment of Mutual Banks. Whoever goes to the mutual bank, and offers real property in pledge, may always obtain money; for the Mutual Bank can issue money to any extent; and that money will always be good, since it is all of it based on actual property, that may be sold under the hammer. The interest will always be at a less rate than 1 per cent per annum, since it covers, not the insurance of the money loaned, there being no such insurance required, as the risk is 0; since it covers, not the damage which is done the bank by keeping it out of its money, as that damage is also 0, the bank having always an un-limited supply remaining on hand, so long as it has a printing-press and paper; since it covers, plainly and simply, the mere expenses of the institution—clerk-hire, rent, paper, printing, etc And it is fair that such expenses should be paid under the form of a rate of interest; for thus each one contributes to bear the expenses of the bank, and in the precise proportion of the benefits he individually experiences from it. Thus the interest, properly so called, is 0; and we venture to predict that the Mutual Bank will one day give all the real credit that will be given; for since this bank will give such at 0 per cent interest per annum, it will be difficult for other institutions to compete with it for any length of time. The day is coming when everything that is bought will be paid for on the spot, and in mu-tual money; when all payments will be made, all wages settled, on the spot The Mutual Bank will never, of course, give personal credit; for it can issue bills only on real credit. It cannot enter into partnership with anybody; for, if it issues bills where there is no real guarantee furnished for their repayment, it vitiates the cur-rency, and renders itself unstable. Personal credit will one day be given by individuals only; that is, capitalists will one day enter into partnership with enterprising and capable men who are with-out capital, and the profits will be divided between the parties ac-cording as their contract of partnership may run. Whoever, in the times of the Mutual Bank, has property, will have money also; and the laborer who has no property will find it very easy to get it; for every capitalist will seek to secure him as a partner All services will then be paid for in ready money; and the demand for labor will be increased three, four and five fold.

As for credit of the kind that is idolized by the present genera-tion, credit which organizes society on feudal principles, confused credit, the Mutual Bank will obliterate it from the face of the earth. Money furnished under the existing system to individuals and corporations is principally applied to speculative purposes, ad-vantageous, perhaps, to those individuals and corporations, if the speculations answer; but generally disadvantageous to the com-munity, whether they answer or whether they fail. If they answer, they generally end in a monopoly of trade, great or small, and in consequent high prices; if they fail, the loss falls on the community. Under the existing system, there is little safety for the merchant. The utmost degree of caution practicable in business has never yet enabled a company or individual to proceed for any long time without incurring bad debts.

The existing organization of credit is the daughter of hard money, begotten upon it incestuously by that insufficiency of circulating medium which results from laws making specie the sole legal tender. The immediate consequences of confused credit are want of confidence, loss of time, commercial frauds, fruitless and repeated applications for payment, complicated with irregular and ruinous expenses. The ultimate consequences are compositions, bad debts, expensive accommodation-loans, lawsuits, insolvency, bankruptcy, separation of classes, hostility, hunger, extravagance, distress, riots, civil war, and, finally, revolution The natural consequences of mutual banking are, first of all, the creation of order, and the definite establishment of due organization in the social body; and, ultimately, the cure of all the evils which flow from the present incoherence and disruption in the relations of production and commerce.

CONCLUSION.

The expensive character of the existing circulating medium is evident on the most superficial inspection. The assessor's valuation for 1830, of the total taxable property then existing in the Commonwealth of Massachusetts, was $208,360,407; the valuation for 1840 was $299,878,329. We may safely estimate, that the valuation for 1850 will be to that of 1840 as that of 1840 was to that of 1830. Performing these calculations, we find that the total amount of taxable property possessed by the people of Massachusetts in the present year, is about $431,588,724.* The excess of this last valuation over that of 1840—i. e , $131,710,395—is the net gain, the clear profit, of the total labor of the people in the ten years under consideration The average profit for each year was, therefore, $13,171,039. In the year 1849, the banks of Massachusetts paid their tax to the state, their losses on bad debts, their rents, their officers and lawyers, and then made dividends of more than SEVEN PER CENT on their capitals. The people, must, therefore, in the course of that year (1840) have paid interest money to the banks to the amount of at least 10 per cent on the whole banking capital of the state. At the close of the year 1848, the banking capital in the state amounted to $32,683,330. Ten per cent on $32,683,330 is $3,268,333—the amount the people paid, during the year 1849, for the use of a currency. If the material of the currency had been iron, $3,268,333 would probably have paid the expenses of the carting and counting. What, then, is the utility of our present paper money? We have estimated the total profits of the whole labor of the people of the Commonwealth for the year 1849, at $13,171,039 It appears, therefore, that the total profits of nearly one-fourth part of the whole population of the state were devoted to the single purpose of paying for the use of a currency.

Mutual Banks would have furnished a much better currency at less than one-tenth of this expense.

The bills of a Mutual Bank cannot reasonably pretend to be standards or measures of value, and this fact is put forth as a recommendation of the mutual money to favorable consideration The silver dollar is the measure and standard of value; and the bills of a Mutual Bank recognize the prior existence of this measure, since they are receivable in lieu of so many silver dollars. The bill of a Mutual Bank is not a measure of value, since it is itself measured and determined in value by the silver dollar. If the dollar rises in value, the bill of the Mutual Bank rises also, since it is receivable in lieu of a silver dollar. The bills

*According to the report of the Valuation Committee, it appears to have been (in the year 1850) $600,000,000—a much larger sum

of a Mutual Bank are not measures of value, but mere instruments of exchange; and, as the value of the mutual money is determined, not by the demand and supply of the mutual money, but by the demand and supply of the precious metals, the Mutual Bank may issue bills to any extent, and those bills will not be liable to any depreciation from excess of supply. And for like reasons, the mutual money will not be liable to rise in value if it happens at any time to be scarce in the market. The issues of said mutual money are therefore susceptible of any contraction or expansion which may be necessary to meet the wants of the community; and such contraction or expansion cannot, by any possibility, be attended with any evil consequence whatever; for the silver dollar, which is the standard of value, will remain throughout at the natural valuation determined for it by the general demand and supply of gold and silver throughout the whole world.

In order that the silver dollar, which is the standard and measure of value, may not be driven out of circulation, the Mutual Bank—which has no vault for specie other than the pockets of the people—ought to issue no bill of a denomination less than five dollars.

THE END,

Milton Keynes UK
Ingram Content Group UK Ltd.
UKHW022301011223
433659UK00005B/68